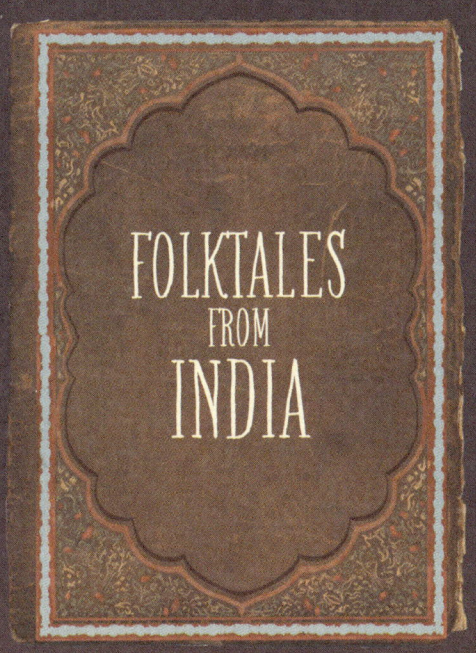

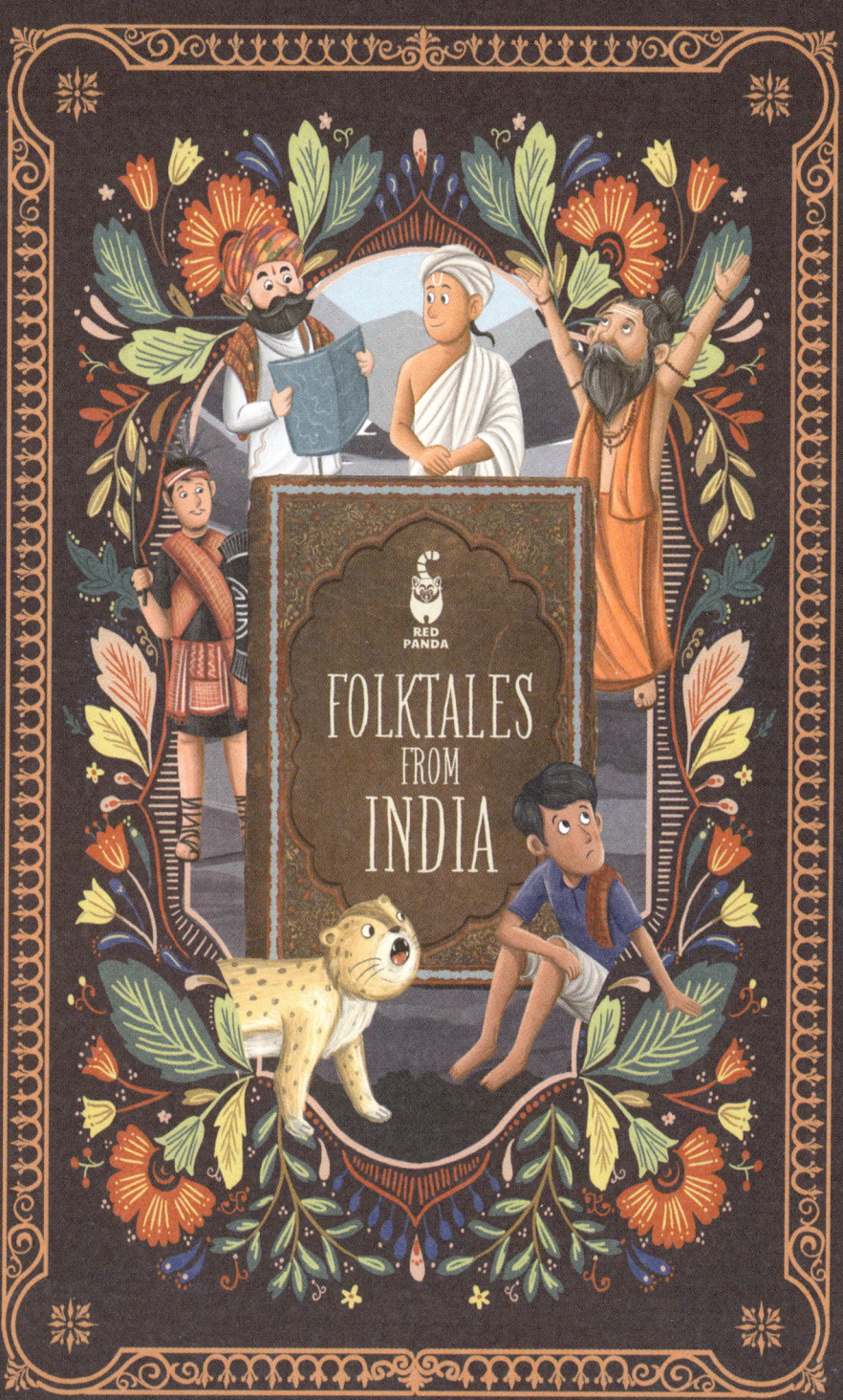

ILLUSTRATED BY NAYAN BOSE

Published by Red Panda, an imprint of Westland Books, a division of Nasadiya Technologies Private Limited, in 2025

No. 269/2B, First Floor, 'Irai Arul', Vimalraj Street, Nethaji Nagar, Alapakkam Main Road, Maduravoyal, Chennai 600095

Westland, the Westland logo, Red Panda and the Red Panda logo are the trademarks of Nasadiya Technologies Private Limited, or its affiliates.

Text and illustrations © Nasadiya Technologies Private Limited, 2025

ISBN: 9789371972222

10 9 8 7 6 5 4 3 2 1

This is a work of fiction. Names, characters, organisations, places, events and incidents are either products of the author's imagination or used fictitiously.

All rights reserved

Book design by Pratik M. Kalekar

Printed at Parksons Graphics Pvt. Ltd

No part of this book may be reproduced, or stored in a retrieval system, or transmitted in any form or by any means, electronic, mechanical, photocopying, recording, or otherwise, without express written permission of the publisher.

FOLKTALES FROM INDIA

Folktales are among the oldest inheritances we carry as a people. Long before books, they travelled as stories told by elders and carried in song and memory. Across India's diverse landscapes, these stories have been told and retold for generations—by firesides, in courtyards, under banyan trees. They shaped how we understood the world, its seasons, its mysteries, its struggles and reminded us who we are.

Rich with cultural detail, alive with the rhythms of place and people, these folktales are more than stories. They are echoes of India's living heritage, inviting readers to journey into the heart of its imagination. Folktales from India are especially rich because they rise from so many landscapes and communities. The snowy mountains of Kashmir, the deserts of Rajasthan, the forests of the North-East, the bustling courts of old cities—all have given birth to their own tales. Each one holds a distinct rhythm, a flavour of its soil, a reflection of its people's way of life.

This collection carries timeless folktales from Kashmir, Himachal, Punjab, Delhi, Assam, Bengal, the North-East and beyond. It is like living archives of culture, weaving together history, imagination and values. The tales celebrate kindness and courage, warn against greed and cruelty and often remind us of our deep connection to nature. Rivers and mountains speak in them, animals teach wisdom and ordinary men and women find extraordinary strength.

In retelling these stories for today's readers, our hope is not only to keep them alive, but also to remind us of the heritage they carry. They belong to all of us—as echoes of our past, mirrors of our present and like beacons, lighting the way into the future.

CONTENTS

1. THE WEAVER'S GIFT — 9
2. THE BEAR AND THE WOODCUTTER — 14
3. RODA AND TOTA — 19
4. BHULI AND THE LEOPARD — 24
5. RANI AND THE DJINN OF FIROZ SHAH KOTLA — 29
6. THE SHEPHERD AND THE WHISPERING DUNES — 34
7. THE FARMER'S MAGICAL POT — 38
8. RAJA SALHES AND THE CROOKED TAXMAN — 43
9. TANI AND THE SUN — 48
10. TEJIMOLA AND THE WHISPERING FLOWERS — 52
11. THE SEVEN SISTERS OF THE SKY — 57
12. THE DIVINE DEER — 61

13. THE MOUNTAIN THAT MOVED  65	14. THE LOTUS TWINS AND THE SORCERESS'S CURSE 69	15. THE RIVER WHO WALKED THE OTHER WAY  74
16. BINDI AND THE SACRED SAL FLOWERS  79		17. THE PEACOCK AND THE SALT MERCHANT OF KUTCH 84
18. THE ORIGIN OF PADDY  89	19. THE LEGEND OF CHILIKA LAKE  94	20. THE BRAVE WASHERWOMAN OF PAITHAN  99
21. THE FARMER AND THE TALKING BULL  104	22. TENALI RAMAN AND THE HORSE SELLER  108	
23. PUNYAKOTI THE TRUTHFUL COW  113	24. THE GIRL WHO FED A STRANGER  118	25. MADHAVAN AND KUTTICHATHAN  123

1. THE WEAVER'S GIFT
A tale from Kashmir

In a quiet village nestled deep in the green valleys of Kashmir, there lived a gentle weaver named Haroon. He lived in a cottage beside the Lidder River, watched over by the snowy mountain peaks.

Haroon was known all across the valley for weaving the softest, warmest pashmina shawls. He used the finest silk threads and dyed them with saffron, walnut bark and wild indigo flowers. His loom clicked and hummed all day, creating shawls with patterns of stars, flowers and birds. Villagers often said that wearing a shawl made by Haroon felt like being wrapped in a soft cloud.

But there was something else that made Haroon special. He never sold his shawls for money. Instead, he gave them away to those who truly needed them. If a widow's fingers grew stiff with cold and she could no longer spin yarn, Haroon would quietly leave a shawl at her doorstep. If a shepherd came down from the mountains with frost on his eyelashes and numb feet, Haroon would greet him with a smile and wrap a warm shawl around his shoulders.

When asked why he gave away what others would sell for good money, Haroon would simply say, 'Cloth warms the body. Kindness warms the soul.'

One year, winter arrived early and hit harder than ever. The winds howled down from the mountains like wolves and snow piled

up high on rooftops. Icy fog crept under doors and clung to windows. Many families in the village had no proper blankets. Their old quilts were torn and thin, and the clay ovens that usually glowed with fire burned low because there was hardly any fuel.

Haroon watched all this quietly from his window. Then, without a word, he opened the wooden chest at the foot of his bed. Inside were all the beautiful shawls he had woven that year. He took out each one, folded them with care and placed them in a basket.

That evening, Haroon walked through the village, his arms full. At each house, he left a shawl on the doorstep. At some homes, he gently wrapped them around sleeping babies. At others, he placed them over the shoulders of old men sitting by fading fires. He found little children shivering and huddled near closed windows and warmed their backs with his shawls.

To everyone, he said only this: 'A gift shared with love is warmer than gold.'

That night, the village sparkled with colour. Pink, blue, green and gold shawls glowed in the soft candlelight. Children stopped crying. Old women smiled through their wrinkles. And though the wind still blew and the snow still fell, everyone felt warmer.

Word of Haroon's kindness spread far beyond the village. It reached the king himself, who lived in a grand palace in Srinagar. The king owned carpets from distant lands, jewel-studded robes and sat on a throne of carved walnut wood.

When he heard of the weaver who gave away his finest shawls without asking for anything in return, the king was puzzled and curious.

'Bring this weaver to me,' the king commanded.

And so Haroon was brought to the palace. The king looked him over and asked, 'Why do you give away your beautiful shawls without taking anything in return?'

Haroon bowed his head gently and replied, 'Your Majesty, kindness cannot be measured in coins. The river gives water to all. The sun shares its light with everyone. I am just doing the same.'

The king sat quietly, thinking. Then he rose from his throne and

THE WEAVER'S GIFT

declared, 'From this day on, when the first snow falls, we shall celebrate a 'Festival of Giving'. Each person shall share something with another, just as the weaver has shared his warmth with the people.'

And so it began. Every year, when snow dusted the trees and rooftops, the valley came alive with giving. People exchanged food, blankets, toys, books and stories. Even the smallest children found something to give—a drawing, a sweet, a smile. The air stayed cold, but hearts were warmed.

And it all began with one kind man, a chest full of shawls and a heart big enough for the whole valley.

In Kashmir, they still say today: 'The warmest gift is the one given from the heart.'

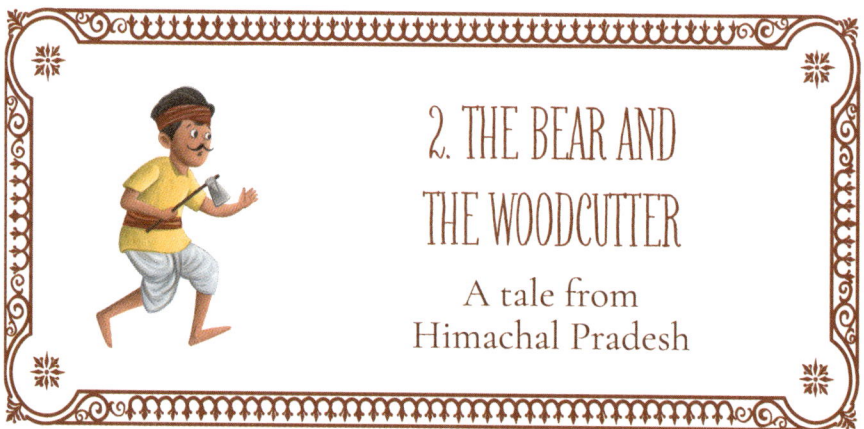

2. THE BEAR AND THE WOODCUTTER
A tale from Himachal Pradesh

High in the Kullu Valley lived a kind-hearted woodcutter named Bhuvan. He rose early every morning, wrapped himself in a thick shawl and climbed the forest slopes with his axe in hand, to cut the trees. He never cut young trees, and only took what he needed. Birds and squirrels followed him as he worked, and he always cared to leave crumbs of roti along the trail.

He lived in a stone cottage on a ridge, where the wind whistled through the cracks in winter. His wife made woollen socks to sell in the market, and his young daughter helped dry apples, tie bundles of firewood and press wildflowers between books. Their life was simple, but their hearts were full.

One cold morning, Bhuvan decided to climb higher than usual in search of dry wood. The forest was still. As he stepped past a patch of deodar trees, he heard a low, rumbling growl.

He froze. Quietly he turned to see where the sound had come from.

Behind a large boulder, half-hidden by snow, a brown Himalayan bear lay trapped in a rusty snare. Its thick paw was caught in the loop of an old hunter's rope. The bear didn't roar or lunge. It only stared at Bhuvan with tired, pained eyes and let out a soft whimper. Bhuvan stepped back in fear, but then paused. The bear wasn't trying to hurt him. It was hurt itself.

Moving carefully, he knelt by the rope, pulled out his axe and began cutting the thick knots. The bear watched but didn't move. When the final knot gave way, the bear slowly pulled its paw free. Dragging its limb, it stood up and turned to look at Bhuvan. Then, without a sound, the bear slipped back into the woods, leaving only pawprints in the snow.

Then one year, winter came early. Snow fell heavy, covering rooftops and blocking paths. The pine trees bowed under the weight of the snow and the stream near the cottage froze solid. The firewood stack was low, and jars of food were sealed shut with ice.

One evening, a storm howled through the valley. The wind pushed against the doors and windows, and cold air slipped through every crack.

'I must find more wood,' Bhuvan said, tying his shawl tightly and reaching for his lantern.

His wife frowned. 'Wait till morning, at least.'

'There may be nothing left by morning,' he said.

'I'll come with you,' said his daughter.

'No,' Bhuvan said. 'Stay warm. I'll be quick.'

He stepped out into the blizzard, his boots crunching through the snow. The forest was silent. Even the birds had gone. Bhuvan walked slowly, his breath puffing in white clouds. Suddenly, he spotted large, round footprints in the snow—too large for a dog or goat.

'A bear?' he murmured. Led by a strange curiosity, he started following the tracks.

It was the bear. Older now, its fur dusted with snow, but it was the same creature he had once freed. The bear looked at him calmly, then turned and walked ahead. Bhuvan hesitated, then followed.

The bear led him along a narrow path, hidden by bushes. At the end of the path was a cave, half-covered with thick branches. Inside, it was dry and warm. In one corner, stacked neatly, were apples, nuts and lumps of honey.

The bear lay down quietly. Bhuvan stepped inside, rested near the fire the bear had built from broken twigs, and warmed his hands. He didn't ask questions. He didn't speak. But in his heart, he knew the forest had remembered.

When the storm passed, Bhuvan returned home carrying a sack full of firewood and a small bundle of food. His wife and daughter cried in relief.

'Where did you find all this?' his daughter asked.

Bhuvan told them the story of the bear he had once rescued, and all that had happened in the forest the night before.

After that, Bhuvan left bowls of honey by the forest edge every spring. Sometimes, he would notice the bowls empty by morning and pawprints in the earth nearby. And the people of Himachal still say 'If you are kind to the forest, the forest will be kind to you.'

3. RODA AND TOTA

A folk tale from Punjab

In a small village in Punjab, where golden wheat fields stretched as far as the eye could see, lived a farmer named Roda. He had a little patch of farmland, a sturdy pair of bullocks and a water well behind his home. But Roda was a lazy man.

While his neighbours rose early to plough the soil, feed the animals and water their fields, Roda preferred to lie under the shade of the old neem tree that stood beside his house. He would sip cool lassi, watching the clouds drift by as birds flew overhead. His fields, once rich with crops, now lay dry and cracked. The plants wilted. The soil sighed. And Roda simply yawned.

One morning, when the village was waking up to the sound of roosters and the clatter of farmers taking to the fields, a travelling merchant arrived. He wore a turban and carried a bamboo cage. Inside was a parrot with bright green feathers that shimmered like emeralds and eyes that sparkled with mischief.

The merchant called out, 'This is Tota! The cleverest parrot in all of Punjab. He speaks, he sings and he brings good luck!' Roda, half-awake under his tree, looked up and smiled. The merchant, amused by his laziness, said, 'He's yours. Let's see if he can teach you something.'

And just like that, Tota became part of Roda's life.

At first, Roda was pleased to have company. He hung the cage on a low branch of a tree beside his house and chatted to the parrot.

'Tota,' he said, scratching his head, 'why don't you fetch water from the well? Or help plough the fields, maybe?'

Tota blinked and squawked, 'You must work for your food!'

Roda chuckled. 'You're just a bird. You can't farm.'

But Tota was no ordinary bird. He watched Roda every day. He saw how poor the fields had grown. The earth had gone dry and started to crack. The crops started to droop in the heat. The birds never came to sing, and even the squirrels had stopped visiting.

One hot summer afternoon, Tota fluttered to the well. He perched on its stone edge and called out to Roda, 'Come, come! The fields are dry and the crops need water!'

Roda, half-asleep, groaned. But the parrot's voice tugged at something inside him. Slowly, he stood up and followed Tota. Together, they filled pots from the well. The water sloshed and spilled, but they walked to the field, and Roda poured the water around the roots.

For the next few days, Roda worked and looked after the crops. The soil no longer looked so tired. Bit by bit, the plants found their colour again. But soon, he returned to his lazy ways. He lay under the neem tree once more, dreaming of sweet mangoes and cool breezes.

Tota knew something had to change. One afternoon, Tota flew up to a high branch and began to sing—not a song, but a story.

'Listen!' he called. 'Once, there was a farmer, just like Roda, who only cared for his own comfort. His fields dried up. His bulls grew thin. But his clever parrot told him: "Work hard, care for your land and it will feed you in return." The farmer listened, and soon, the fields turned green again. He had enough to eat, enough to share and enough to rest without shame.'

The villagers paused their work. A few children gathered under the neem tree, and an old man nodded thoughtfully. Roda sat up, his cheeks warm with embarrassment.

RODA AND TOTA

He looked at Tota and said softly, 'You're right. I've been lazy. My land is not to be wasted. I must care for it like it once cared for me.'

From that day, Roda rose with the sun and stepped into the fields. He sowed seeds and took good care of the plants. His bullocks worked happily beside him. And Tota stayed close, singing, chirping or simply watching with pride. The crops grew tall and strong. The land stayed happy and the harvest was kind. Because when we care for the earth, and when we listen to those who speak with love and wisdom, life always finds a way to bloom.

4. BHULI AND THE LEOPARD

A brave tale from Kumaon, Uttarakhand

High in the misty hills of Kumaon, lined with pine and oak trees, lived a brave young girl named Bhuli. Her village sat on a steep slope, with stone houses and narrow winding paths between fields of maize and millet.

Bhuli was known across the village for her sharp wit and fearless spirit. She lived with her parents and younger brother, Puran, in a small house near the edge of the forest.

One clear afternoon, after helping her mother grind grain, Bhuli took Puran for a walk. 'Let's pick some wild berries,' she said, swinging a small basket on her arm. 'But don't wander too far.'

They walked through the tall grass, laughing as they chased butterflies. Kokila, the cuckoo's call rang across the trees, light and cheerful. Puran found a ripe red berry and held it up. 'This one's for you!' he said.

Bhuli smiled. 'You're getting good at this.'

They kept walking, just a little deeper into the woods than usual. Bhuli looked up at the sky and saw that the sky was starting to fade. 'We should head back soon,' she said.

They started walking back to the village. Suddenly Puran stopped in his tracks.

'Did you hear that?' he whispered.

BHULI AND THE LEOPARD

Bhuli turned. A branch cracked behind them. Then, from behind an old oak tree, a fearsome leopard stepped out.

'Little ones,' it rumbled, its voice deep like thunder through the hills. 'You've wandered too far. I haven't eaten in days.'

Its amber eyes stared straight at them. It crept closer with each step.

Puran gasped and stepped back. Bhuli's heart pounded, but she didn't move. She looked at Puran, frozen in fear, and then at the leopard. Suddenly, a clever idea came to her.

'O great leopard,' she said, trying to keep her calm. 'You're strong. But I know where you'll find better food.'

The leopard tilted its head. It didn't move, but it was listening.

Bhuli took a small step sideways, putting herself between Puran and the leopard. 'Follow me,' she said. 'Just a little further. There's something waiting for you.'

'This better not be a trick, girl,' it growled. 'If I don't like what I find, I'll eat you first.'

Slowly and carefully, she started walking, leading the leopard towards a narrow trail she remembered from her walks with her father. 'Don't move, Puran,' she whispered as she passed him.

Bhuli moved steadily, and the leopard followed. Her palms were sweaty, and her legs felt weak, but she kept walking.

She led the leopard towards a rocky ledge where wild rhododendron bushes grew thick. Standing by the edge, Bhuli turned and began to sing a slow, familiar tune—a song of the mountains, a tune taught to her by village elders. She remembered the stories of how the song summoned the forest spirits that came to help people in times of trouble.

The leopard paused in confusion, eyes fixed on her. As the song went on, the tiger stood still, mesmerized by the magic of the song.

Bhuli slowly reached down and picked up a stone. Then another. She tossed them near the leopard's feet. The sound startled it. The leopard gave a low growl, then turned its head and looked

back towards the forest. After a few long seconds, it slipped away into the trees.

Bhuli stood frozen until she was sure it was gone. Then she ran back.

Puran stood right where she'd left him, eyes wide. As soon as he saw her, he burst into tears. 'I thought—it was going to eat us!'

Bhuli hugged him tightly. 'It's gone. We're safe.'

They hurried home without stopping. When they reached the village, Bhuli told her parents what had happened. Neighbours gathered to listen. Everyone was amazed.

From then on, the story of Bhuli and the leopard was told again and again. Parents reminded their children not to stray too far, but they also told them that quick thinking and love could be stronger than fear.

Each spring, when the rhododendrons bloom red on the slopes and the Kokila sings from the treetops, the people of the hills remember the girl who stood between danger and her little brother —not with a stick or a sword, but with courage and cleverness.

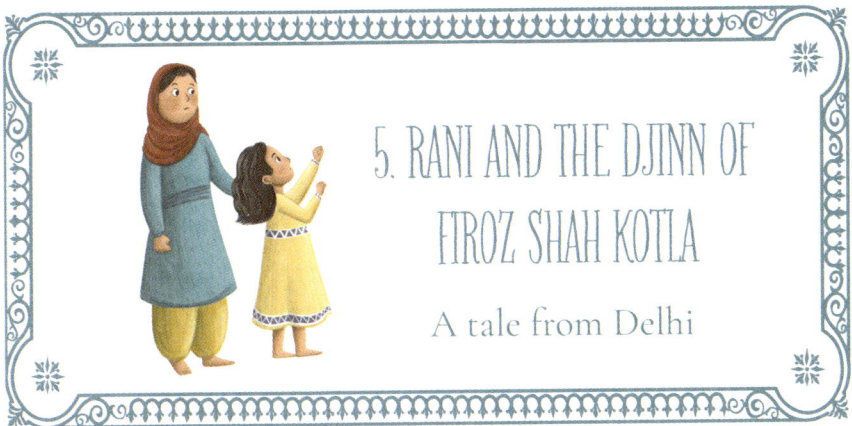

5. RANI AND THE DJINN OF FIROZ SHAH KOTLA

A tale from Delhi

In a time when the Yamuna flowed clear and the city of Delhi was young, a great grey fort stood tall by the riverbank. The Firoz Shah Kotla Fort was once the pride of a mighty Sultan, but over the years, the city grew around it and the fort began to crumble. Yet, the people of Delhi still came on Thursdays. They believed the old fort was home to djinns—magical beings made of smokeless fire.

Among the many djinns, one was kinder than the rest. His name was Nanhe Miyan. Some said he was as tall as a tree. Others said he could turn into wind and listen through walls. But all agreed on one thing: if you wrote to Nanhe Miyan with a true heart, he would listen.

In a narrow alley of Old Delhi, there lived a girl named Rani. She was small for her age but clever and kind. Her father was a rickshaw puller and her mother sewed buttons in the market. They did not have much, but they had a happy home. Every evening, they gathered for dinner, laughing and talking about each other' day.

One day, Rani's younger brother came down with a burning fever. He tossed and turned on his bed, and could not eat a thing. Rani hurried to fetch the neighbourhood doctor, who came at once. He shook his head in worry, and said that the boy should be given a

rare medicine, that could only be found in a clinic far away. But the medicine cost more than her parents could earn in a month. That night, the family sat around the dinner table in silence. Rani sat by the lamp, thinking hard. Then she remembered what the bangle-seller had said at the market, 'If your heart is pure, write to Nanhe Miyan on a Thursday. The djinn listens.'

The next morning, Rani took a piece of paper, and carefully wrote a letter. She began, 'Dear Nanhe Miyan, my brother is sick. My parents are worried. Please help us. Please, I promise I'll share whatever I can with others if only he gets well. Yours, Rani.'

She folded the letter and walked to the old fort with her mother. The ruins felt ancient and quiet, but not empty. She climbed the worn steps of the mosque and tucked her letter into a crack in the wall, beside many others. Candles flickered. The scent of rose water and incense hung in the air.

'He will hear,' her mother whispered, and they walked home.

The next evening, they heard a gentle knock at the door. Rani opened the door and saw a tall man in a pale white kurta with a kind smile. He said, 'I am from the clinic nearby. Someone has left medicine for your son, already paid for. It was marked for the girl who wrote to Nanhe Miyan.'

Rani looked at her mother in disbelief, their faces breaking into wide smiles as relief washed over them. Rani's mother wept with joy. The medicine worked, and by the week's end, her brother was running around the courtyard once more.

Rani remembered her promise. She shared her school lunch with a hungry classmate and gave her only pencil to a boy who had none. She never saw the tall man again.

Years passed. Rani got married, and had children of her own. Every once in a while, she would visit the fort with her children. She would tell them, 'If you write with a true heart, Nanhe Miyan will listen. And remember, the magic works strongest when kindness leads the way.'

And sometimes, when the breeze stirred the leaves and carried the scent of rose water and old stone, her children would smile, wondering if Nanhe Miyan was nearby watching, listening and keeping his promise.

6. THE SHEPHERD AND THE WHISPERING DUNES

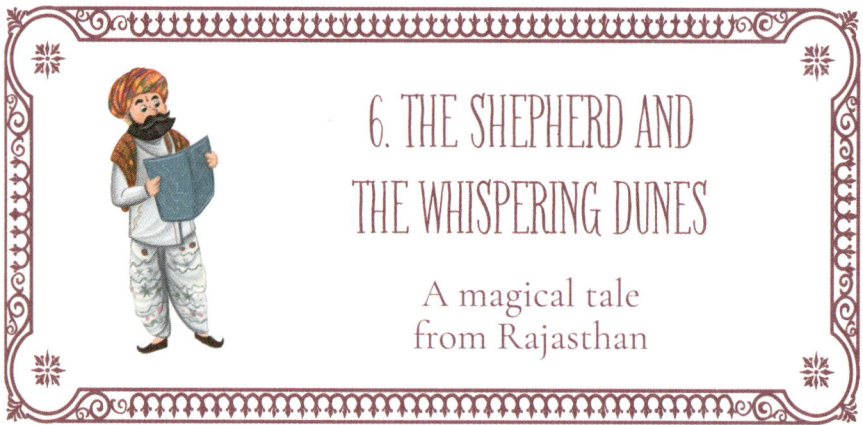

A magical tale from Rajasthan

Under the blazing sun of Rajasthan, where the earth cracked like dry clay and the air smelled of dust and spices, lived a young shepherd named Kalu. He was only ten, but he knew every twist and turn of the sandy land like the back of his hand.

One afternoon, the sun beat down fiercely. Kalu led his sheep and goats towards a faraway waterhole. The soft bleating of his flock mixed with the crunch of their hooves on the dry ground. Suddenly, something caught his eye. Not far away, a large carriage was stuck in the middle of the desert, with its wheels jammed deep in the sand. Two tired horses snorted and stamped, struggling to pull it free.

A worried man stood beside the carriage. He wore fine clothes and a fancy turban. In his hands was a map. He turned it this way and that, but it only seemed to make him more puzzled.

'Oh no, oh no!' he said, wiping sweat from his face. 'This map shows a straight path to Udaipur, but all I see is endless sand!'

Kalu moved his flock closer. The man noticed him and called out sharply, 'Boy, do you know the way to Udaipur? Why does this map show a path where there is only desert?'

Kalu looked at the map and then at the dunes. His voice was calm. 'This map is for the winter months, sir.'

THE SHEPHERD AND THE WHISPERING DUNES

'Winter months?' the man asked, frowning. 'How does that matter?' Kalu smiled. 'In winter, the rains fill the dry riverbeds. They become hard and easy to walk on. But in summer, those riverbeds turn soft and sandy. The shortest path in winter is the hardest now.'

The man shook his head. 'A path is a path,' he said. He pulled at the carriage, but it sank deeper.

Kalu waited quietly. 'The best way now is over the high dunes,' he said. 'The wind makes the sand firmer there. Listen to the crows. They always fly towards water.'

The man laughed. 'You want me to trust a crow's call instead of my map?'

'The desert has its own secrets,' Kalu said softly. 'And the crows know them well.'

The man sighed. His carriage was stuck and he was tired. 'Alright, boy,' he said. 'Show me the way. But if we get lost, you will be in trouble.'

Kalu smiled and hitched his strong goat, Bholu, to the carriage. He pointed to the firmer dunes ahead. With the flock moving gently before them, they set off slowly. The sun sank low, painting the sky with bright reds and purples.

At last, just as the daylight began to fade, they reached a sparkling waterhole. The cool water glistened in the moonlight. Beyond it, the lights of Udaipur twinkled softly.

The man stared in wonder. 'You found the way,' he said. 'Not with my map, but by listening to the sand and the crows.'

Kalu nodded and bowed. 'The desert speaks, sir, if you learn to listen.' He unhitched Bholu and led his flock to drink.

That day, the man learned something important. Sometimes, the best wisdom is not found in books or maps but in the quiet knowledge of those who live close to the earth. And Kalu, the young shepherd, kept guiding his flock. His heart was as wide as the sky and as patient as the desert winds.

7. THE FARMER'S MAGICAL POT

A timeless tale from Uttar Pradesh

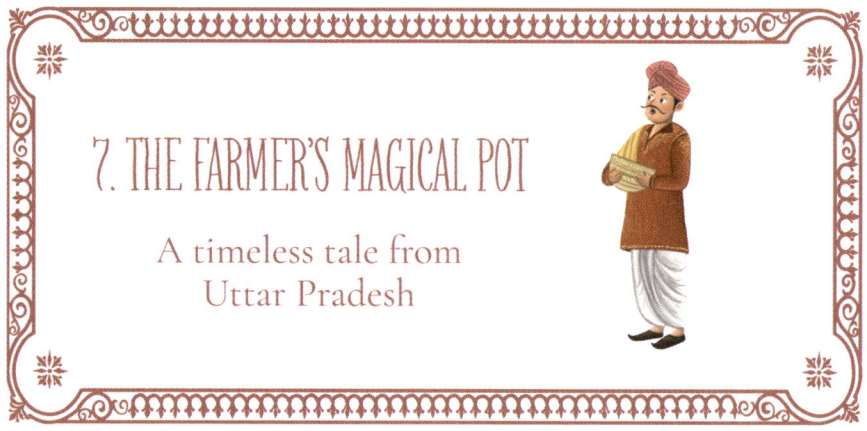

In the fertile plains of Uttar Pradesh, where mustard fields stretched like golden carpets and the Yamuna River wound through villages, there lived a poor farmer named Govind. His small hut stood amid green fields at the edge of Mathura. The sweet fragrance of jasmine and the smell of freshly tilled soil always filled the air around his modest home.

Govind worked tirelessly in his tiny patch of land, but the rains had been poor for three seasons. The soil had started cracking and his wheat stalks stood barely knee-high, with their heads drooping. His wife, Radha, often went to bed hungry so their young son, Arjun, could have an extra roti.

Govind started to worry about his crop. 'If I don't find a way to water the fields, this season's harvest will be as good as none.' One evening, he decided to dig a new well behind his hut. He worked steadily, scooping out the dry soil. Suddenly, his spade struck something hard with a loud clang. Brushing away the earth, he uncovered a small brass pot, its surface covered in intricate patterns.

'Radha, come quickly!' he called out, his voice echoing across the courtyard.

Radha emerged from the kitchen, wiping her hands on her cotton dupatta.

THE FARMER'S MAGICAL POT

'Look what I found!' Govind held up the pot, which felt surprisingly warm despite being buried in cool earth.

Radha examined it carefully, running her fingers over the carved peacocks and lotus flowers. 'It's beautiful, but we need food, not fancy pots.'

That night, as the family sat around their small clay stove, Arjun looked up at his father with large, hopeful eyes. 'Papa, I'm so hungry. Do we have anything else to eat?'

Govind's heart ached. He looked at the brass pot sitting in the corner and whispered, 'I wish we had enough rice to fill our bellies.'

Suddenly, the pot began to glow with a soft, golden light. Steam rose from its mouth, carrying the delicious aroma of perfectly cooked basmati rice. The family watched in wonder as the pot filled to the brim with fluffy, fragrant rice.

'It's magic!' gasped Arjun, clapping his hands with delight.

Radha cautiously touched the pot's rim. 'Govind, this cannot be real.'

But the rice was indeed real, and it was the most delicious they had ever tasted. From that day forward, Govind would make a wish whenever the family was hungry, and the pot would provide exactly what they needed.

News of the magical pot spread through the village like wildfire. Soon, neighbours began arriving at Govind's door, their faces bony with hunger.

'Please, Govind bhai,' pleaded his neighbour, Ramu. 'My children haven't eaten in two days. Can your pot help us?'

Without hesitation, Govind welcomed them in. 'Of course, come sit. Magical pot, please provide food for all our guests.'

The pot glowed brighter and produced enough dal, rice and vegetables to feed everyone. Word spread further, and soon, people from neighbouring villages were making the journey to Govind's humble home.

One day, a rich zamindar named Thakur Bhanu Singh heard about the pot. His eyes glittered with greed as he thought about the

pot that never ran out of food. He rode up to Govind's hut on his decorated horse, flanked by armed guards.

'Farmer!' he barked, dismounting with a heavy thud. 'I demand you give me that pot immediately. A precious thing like that shouldn't belong to a lowly peasant.'

Govind stood his ground, though his knees trembled. 'Thakur sahib, the pot chooses to help the hungry. It cannot be owned by anyone.'

'Nonsense!' Bhanu Singh snatched the pot from Govind's hands. 'Pot, I command you to fill with gold coins!'

The pot remained cold and empty. Furious, the zamindar shook it violently. 'Give me diamonds! Give me pearls!'

Still nothing. In his rage, Bhanu Singh hurled the pot to the ground. It shattered into a thousand pieces, each fragment turning to dust and blowing away in the wind.

'You've destroyed it!' cried Radha, tears streaming down her face.

But Govind smiled gently and knelt where the pot had broken. As he touched the earth, a small mango sapling sprouted from the ground. 'The pot's magic hasn't died,' he said softly. 'It has simply changed form.'

The mango tree grew with miraculous speed, and within days, it was heavy with sweet, juicy fruits. The tree provided sweet mangoes for the entire village, and its branches offered shade to weary travellers. Even today, people say that if you sit beneath a mango tree and share your food with someone hungry, you'll receive the same blessing that Govind discovered long ago.

The greedy zamindar, meanwhile, found that his wealth began to disappear, coin by coin, until he was left with nothing but the wisdom that true magic lies not in taking, but in giving.

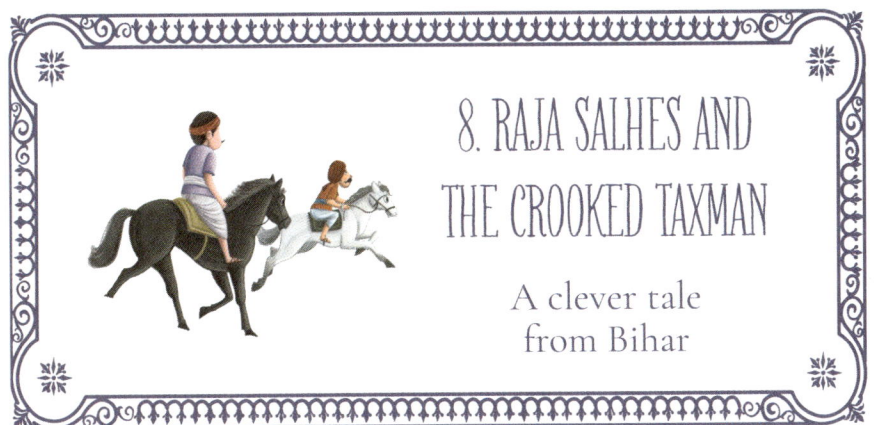

8. RAJA SALHES AND THE CROOKED TAXMAN

A clever tale from Bihar

Long ago, the kingdom of Mithila was ruled by the great Raja Salhes. He was a humble king without a grand palace or a crown. But he was brave, and he was kind. He stood up for the weak, and his courage gave them strength.

His name was known in every home of Mithila. People remembered his courage and spoke of him with affection. Everyone knew that if trouble came, Salhes would come to rescue them.

But not all was well in those peaceful villages. In a dusty corner of Mithila lived a man named Daroga Singh. He was the tax collector, but he was known for collecting more than his fair share. He snatched sacks of rice, bundles of lentils, even a farmer's last block of jaggery.

Evenings turned quiet in the village. Mothers whispered worries and fathers stared at bare grain jars. With heavy hearts, they lit small lamps and prayed: 'Will Salhes hear us?'

Their prayers did not go unanswered. One morning, the villagers woke up to the sound of hoofbeats. It was Pavan, Salhes's snow-white horse. Salhes sat tall on Pavan's back, wrapped in a simple red angavastram. A crowd gathered around him.

'Raja,' one old woman said, her voice trembling, 'Daroga takes even the rice meant for our children.'

A farmer stepped forward holding his empty basket. 'He demanded my last block of jaggery,' he said. 'What shall we eat now?'

A young mother clutched her child to her chest. 'Even the lentils I saved for the baby, he carried away,' she whispered.

One boy blurted out, eyes flashing with anger, 'He left us with nothing, Raja! Not even a fistful of grain.'

Another villager added, 'He comes with guards. Who dares to say no?'

Salhes listened in silence, his hand resting on Pavan's mane. His eyes scanned the faces of the villagers, and he knew. Without a word, he turned Pavan towards the taxman's grand house.

Daroga Singh was lounging on a charpai, eating syrupy balushahi, when Salhes arrived. Daroga Singh raised an eyebrow.

'What brings the peasant king to my court?' he asked, licking his fingers.

Salhes stepped forward. 'You've drained these people like dry wells. Return what is not yours.'

Daroga Singh laughed. 'I take what the law allows. Who are you to stop me?'

The sun blinked through the neem trees as Salhes answered, 'Let the land decide. We shall race. If I win, you return every grain. If you win, I'll double what the villagers owe you.'

The taxman smirked. 'Prepare to pay, forest hero.'

Crows called from the rooftops the next morning as the village gathered. The path was set—down to the banyan tree near the river bend, and back again. Daroga Singh rode a sleek black horse, groomed like a bridegroom. Salhes, calm as a still pond, mounted Pavan.

A boy clapped. The race began.

Daroga Singh bolted ahead, hooves thundering. Villagers gasped. But Pavan moved like mist, gliding through sugarcane and mustard. When Daroga Singh reached the tree, Salhes was already there, brushing dust from his shoulder.

'Impossible!' Daroga Singh cried out. 'You cheated!'

RAJA SALHES AND THE CROOKED TAXMAN

Salhes shook his head. 'While you followed the beaten path, I trusted the fields. A true leader knows his land, and a true cause finds its own way.'

There was no arguing with that. Daroga Singh returned every stolen grain, lentil and coin. That evening, laughter returned to the village. Smoke from litti-chokha drifted through the air, and children danced while elders sang old songs with full bellies.

And as the stars appeared, the villagers spoke not just of Salhes's speed, but his wisdom. They remembered how justice did not shout but arrived with quiet courage.

9. TANI AND THE SUN

A tale from Arunachal Pradesh

In the misty hills of Arunachal Pradesh, where orchids bloom wild and the forests hum with the sound of cicadas, lived a boy named Tani. He belonged to the Adi tribe, known for their bamboo houses on stilts and colourful dances during the Solung festival.

Tani was a curious boy who loved to explore the green slopes that stretched out behind his house. He would run around all day, skipping through the rocks, streams and muddy paths. These paths wound through the forest near his village, where giant ferns brushed his arms and monkeys swung through the trees. But there was one thing he didn't like—the sun.

'It's too hot!' he would complain. 'My neck burns when I go to fetch water and the ground cracks in the fields.'

One afternoon, while sitting beneath a broad-leafed tree, Tani had an idea. 'What if I trap the sun?' he thought. 'Then it will stop bothering us with all its heat.'

Tani ran to his house and picked the strongest bamboo from his family's store. He weaved a large cage, tying the ends with cane ropes and whispering a small forest chant he had heard from the elders. Before dawn, he crept up a high hill where the sun first rose and put his trap in place, hiding behind a mossy rock.

TANI AND THE SUN

As the first golden rays stretched across the sky, the sun came up slowly, yawning behind the clouds. Just as it peeked over the hill, Tani pulled the trap's string. Snap! The bamboo trap sprang shut.

The sun was caught. At first, Tani shrieked with joy. The sky turned grey, and the heat faded. No more sweating, no more dusty feet. He danced his way back to the village, glad to be rid of the sun.

But soon, the wind stopped blowing. The birds stopped singing. The flowers drooped and closed. The river slowed to a trickle, and smoke from the kitchen fires curled without lifting. In the dark, people stumbled and bumped into one another. Grandmothers couldn't find herbs. Hunters couldn't track footprints. Children began to cry.

Back in his home, Tani sat in silence. He missed the chirping of birds and the smell of rice boiling over wood fires. Without the sun, the world felt cold and sad.

The village elders gathered in the dark. One of them whispered to the others that he had seen Tani climbing the hill with the trap. They lit pine torches and called Tani. 'Why did you trap the Sun, child?'

Tani looked down. 'I only wanted to stop the heat.'

An old woman placed her hand on his shoulder, smiling. 'The sun gives us warmth and light. Without it, nothing can grow.'

Tani nodded slowly. 'I'll fix it,' he whispered.

He ran up the hill and opened the trap. The sun, though slightly crumpled, stretched out and rose into the sky with a fiery grin. The light returned. Birds chirped again. Flowers opened. Laughter filled the village.

That evening, as the sky turned soft orange and pink, the villagers gathered for their evening meal. Tani sat quietly near the fire.

'I understand now,' he said. 'Too much heat is hard. But no sun at all is worse.'

The elder smiled. 'Nature needs balance. The sun, the rain, the wind—all have their time and place.'

And so, in the valleys of Arunachal Pradesh, where the hills blush at sunrise and children play beneath golden rays, Tani's tale is still told. It reminds everyone that even a clever idea must follow the ways of the world.

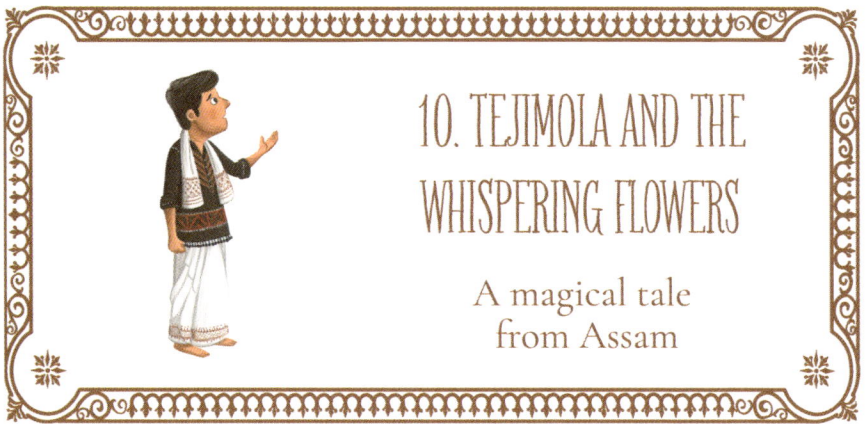

10. TEJIMOLA AND THE WHISPERING FLOWERS

A magical tale from Assam

Once upon a time, in a bright little village in Assam, lived a cheerful girl named Tejimola. She was a kind-hearted girl, always ready to help her neighbours and care for those around her. Her mother had passed away when she was very young, leaving her father to care for her alone. He was a travelling merchant, who loved her more than anything in the world.

After several years, he married a woman from the nearby village. One day soon after, her father had to go on a long journey to a far-off market. He left Tejimola with his new wife, hoping she would have a kind woman to care for her. But the new stepmother was cold and unkind. She was jealous of Tejimola's goodness, and every time Tejimola smiled, the stepmother grew angry.

'You'll do all the chores now,' she snapped. 'Water the garden, sweep the floor, pound the rice and no complaining!'

Tejimola obeyed in silence. From dawn till dusk, she worked like a slave. Her little hands turned red from scrubbing, her feet got dusty from running to the well. But still, she sang softly to herself and looked to the horizon, hoping her father would return.

Then one cruel morning, the stepmother's anger turned into something far worse. She grew angry when Tejimola forgot to bring water from the well. She flew at the girl in rage and gave her a tight

TEJIMOLA AND THE WHISPERING FLOWERS

slap. Tejimola fell still. The house went quiet. And just like that, Tejimola's kind spirit slipped away—light as a butterfly.

'Good riddance,' muttered the stepmother, dusting her hands.

But Tejimola's spirit wandered around the house, free at last from her stepmother's cruelty.

From the soft earth of the backyard, a lovely gourd plant sprang up. Its leaves were deep green, and its gourds sparkled in the sun. A few days later, Tejimola's father came home from his travels. He looked around and asked, 'Where is my daughter?' The stepmother folded her hands and said quickly, 'She went away suddenly one day. I don't know where,' Then he saw the gourd plant in the backyard. Suddenly he felt something stir inside him.

'What a beautiful plant,' he whispered. 'Why does it feel like my daughter is near?'

The stepmother heard this, and grew restless. 'It's just a silly weed,' she said, yanking it out and tossing it away.

But Tejimola's spirit was strong.

Next, she became a lemon tree near the village path. Its fruits were golden and fragrant, bursting with juice. People stopped to admire it. The father walked past one day and picked a lemon.

'This scent,' he said softly, 'why does it remind me of my daughter?'

The stepmother saw villagers praising the tree and grew angry once more. She took an axe and chopped it down.

Yet still, Tejimola's spirit did not give up.

This time, she became a tiny bird with shimmering feathers and a song like the river's song in spring. Once she saw her father tying up a sack of spices in the courtyard. She flew to the rooftop and began to sing a melody. Her father suddenly looked up to see the bird singing. The song reached deep into his heart.

'Tejimola?' he whispered. 'Is it really you?'

He held out his hand. The bird flew down, landed gently, and gazed into his eyes. At that moment, he knew. His daughter was still with him.

The stepmother screamed, fuming at the sight. 'Away with you,

you cursed bird!' But the bird only flew to a quiet pond nearby and settled on a glowing lotus.

The father followed the bird with his heart pounding. As he touched the shining flower, the air shimmered. The lotus opened, and from it rose Tejimola—smiling, alive and full of light.

'Father!' she cried, running into his arms.

'My child!' he wept, holding her close.

The stepmother watched, her face pale. Tears welled in her eyes. She had never seen such love, and for the first time, she felt shame.

'I... I'm sorry,' she whispered. 'I was wrong.'

Tejimola looked at her and gave a quiet smile.

'Kindness always finds its way back,' she said.

People in the village never forgot what had happened. Tejimola's story was passed down through generations. And every spring, when lemon blossoms bloom and birds sing at dawn, many believe it's Tejimola's spirit, gently reminding them to choose love over cruelty.

11. THE SEVEN SISTERS OF THE SKY

A tale from Meghalaya

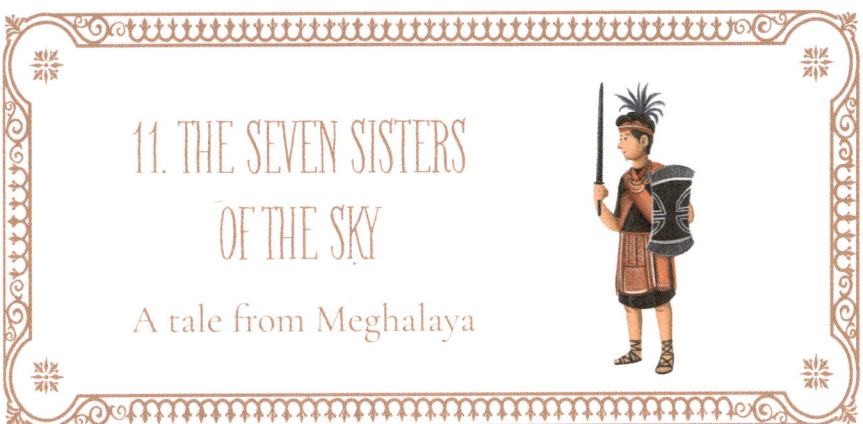

High in the misty hills of Meghalaya, thick clouds wrapped around the Khasi and Jaintia mountains. Along its valleys lived Rinu, a poor farmer who worked his little patch of paddy fields. He spent his days bent over the soil, planting, weeding and carrying water. People in the village knew him for his kindness, for he often shared his harvest with neighbours who had less. Often, he worked until his back hurt and his eyes grew heavy.

One evening, Rinu lay down beside his fields looking up at the wide night sky, tired after a long day of work. Just then, the stars above seemed to stir. Rinu watched in awe as a star slowly started coming down from the skies. Then another followed. And another. One by one, seven glowing lights slowly floated down from the heavens. As they touched the earth, the lights shimmered and took human form. They were seven beautiful sisters, dressed in sparkling white robes.

'We have come to help you,' said the eldest sister, with a gentle smile. 'Your kindness to the land has reached the spirits above.'

From the next day, the sisters began to work alongside Rinu, planting paddy and watering the fields with water from the clear mountain streams. Their laughter echoed through the hills. Soon, the

land turned green and heavy with grain, and the fruit trees bent low with plenty of fruit. In no time, news spread of Rinu's good fortune.

One day, the king's tax collectors arrived. Seeing the fields bursting with harvest, they demanded an impossible sum of grain. Rinu fell to his knees. 'If I give you all this, my village will starve,' he pleaded. But the men only laughed and said they would return at sunrise. That night, Rinu sat by his field, head in his hands. The sisters came to him. The eldest said, 'You have cared for the land and shared with your people. Do not lose hope.' Together, the seven sisters began to sing. Their voices rose like the wind through the hills, and the rice stalks shimmered with light. By morning, the fields had multiplied, golden and endless.

When the tax collectors finally arrived, they marched straight into Rinu's fields with baskets and carts. They laughed at the farmer, saying, 'This will not take long.' One by one, they began cutting the stalks and loading them high. Soon their carts overflowed, but when they turned to look, the fields still swayed full and heavy with rice.

'Faster!' one of them shouted, and the men worked harder, their arms aching from the load. Yet no matter how many stalks they cut, the fields did not shrink. The harvest seemed endless. Sweat rolled down their faces, and still the golden rice stood tall.

The men dropped their sickles in fear. 'This is no ordinary land,' one whispered. Without another word, they abandoned their carts and hurried back the way they had come, too shaken to even look behind them. From that day, no collector ever dared to trouble Rinu's village again.

But the sisters knew their time on earth was ending. One evening, as the first stars appeared, they said farewell. 'Remember, abundance is safe only when it is shared.' Slowly, they rose into the sky, becoming the constellation of the Seven Sisters.

Rinu never forgot their words. Each season, he gave the first basket of rice to his neighbours, teaching others that when people work together and share what they have, the land itself gives back.

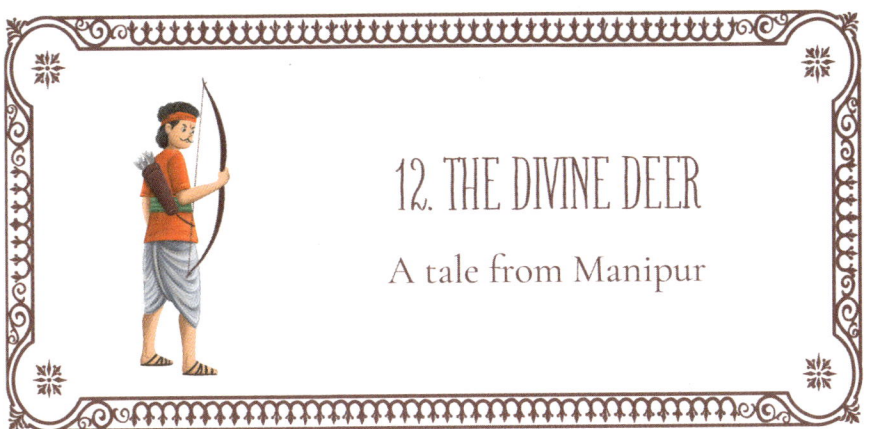

12. THE DIVINE DEER

A tale from Manipur

Deep in the forests of Manipur, where bamboo groves whispered secrets and orchids bloomed in soft shades of pink and white, lived a young hunter named Thoiba. Thoiba had a bold heart, facing wild boars, bears and even leopards without a trace of fear. One misty morning, he set out for the forest with his bow and quiver. He wandered farther through the trees than he had ever been before, chasing a golden pheasant. Tall trees rose all around like giants, their leaves shimmering with drops of dew.

Suddenly, Thoiba realised he was lost. The familiar paths had vanished and sunlight barely touched the forest floor through the thick canopy. He wandered this way and that, but no matter how far he walked, he could not find the path back home.

Just then, from behind a grove of bamboo, a magnificent deer appeared. Its coat gleamed like silk and its antlers curved like branches of a tree. The deer's eyes shone in the dim light, as if they were trying to tell him something.

'Follow me,' the deer seemed to say, turning slowly and stepping lightly over moss and fallen leaves.

Thoiba stopped in his tracks. 'How can I follow you?' he muttered. 'You're only an animal. What if you lead me deeper into danger?'

The deer lifted its head and looked straight at him. Its voice was soft, like wind rustling through bamboo leaves. 'I do not wish

you harm. The forest is wide, and its paths are many. Alone, you will wander in circles. With me, you will find the way.'

Thoiba's grip on his bow loosened. He studied the shining eyes once more. Something in their calm made his doubts fade. Slowly, he nodded. 'Very well. I'll trust you.'

He followed through winding paths and sparkling streams. They walked past ancient stones carved with symbols of forest spirits. The deer moved gracefully without looking back.

Along the way, Thoiba noticed small signs, such as the songs of birds, the rustle of leaves and the scent of wildflowers, guiding their steps. He began to feel a deep respect for the forest's quiet power.

At last, the deer stopped near the edge of the forest, where Thoiba could see smoke rising from his village. The deer bowed its head and then vanished silently among the trees.

Thoiba looked back with gratitude. He had learned that the forest was not just a place to hunt but a living home full of spirits that watched over all who lived there.

From that day on, Thoiba honoured the forest. He spoke softly to the trees, left gifts of fruit for the spirits and never took more than he needed.

13. THE MOUNTAIN THAT MOVED

A tale from Mizoram

In the green hills of Mizoram, there was once a small village named Lunglei. The villagers lived in colourful houses with thatched roofs and bamboo walls. Their days began with the beating of the traditional drums called khuang and the sweet scent of pai flowers that grew wild on the hills.

But there was a problem. A great mountain stood so close to the village that it blocked the sunlight for much of the day. The warm sun rays never reached the rice fields or the gardens where the villagers grew their vegetables. Without sunlight, the plants drooped and the children missed the bright days playing in the courtyards.

That evening, some of the villagers sat together by the rice fields, watching the pale, weak plants bend low.

'Look at the stalks,' said Lalthanga, shaking his head. 'They should be tall and strong by now, but without sunlight they barely grow.'

A young mother added softly, 'Even my little garden of beans has dried up. What will I feed the children when the harvest fails?'

The village potter sighed. 'And without grain, who will trade with me? Soon the store jars will be empty.'

The group fell silent for a while, listening to the rustle of the bamboo groves. Then an elder spoke in a low voice. 'If this continues, we will face a season of hunger. The mountain blocks not only the

sun but also our future.'

Anxious murmurs spread among them. The worry in their eyes was clear—unless something changed, the whole village would suffer.

One morning, an old woman from the village named Lalruatfeli, called the people together. 'We must ask the mountain to move,' she said gently. 'If we pay our respect to Mother Earth and pray with all our hearts, the mountain might listen.'

The villagers gathered at the foot of the mountain, wearing their colourful puanchei clothes and traditional necklaces made of beads and shells. They lit incense made from the fragrant chhipchhi wood and began to sing prayers.

Their voices rose up the slopes, echoing among the trees. Birds stopped to listen. The bamboo swayed softly as if nodding in agreement.

For three days and nights, the villagers prayed without stopping. They asked the mountain kindly to give space to the sun and the crops.

On the fourth morning, as the first golden light spread over the hills, something amazing happened. Slowly, the mountain began to move. Inch by inch, it shifted away, sliding across the earth like a giant rolling log.

The villagers watched in wonder as the mountain made way for the sun. Warm rays filled the village and the fields. The rice turned green and strong, the flowers opened wide and the children laughed as they played under the bright blue sky.

From that day, the mountain stayed in its new place, far enough to let the sun shine on the village. The villagers never forgot to thank it with prayers and offerings of fresh fruit and zu—a sweet rice drink.

The story of the moving mountain is still told in Mizoram, where the hills are alive with music and the air smells of wet earth and wild flowers. It reminds everyone that prayer and respect for nature can change the world in the most wonderful ways.

14. THE LOTUS TWINS AND THE SORCERESS'S CURSE

A clever tale from West Bengal

Once upon a time in Bengal, there lived a kind King and Queen. Their kingdom was famous for its gentle rivers and bustling markets, full of delicious sandesh. The people of the kingdom loved their rulers, for they were just and gentle. Yet the royal couple carried one sorrow in their hearts—they had no children. They longed for children.

Every morning the queen offered flowers at the temple and prayed for a child. Every evening the king lit a lamp by the river and asked the gods to bless their home. At last, their prayers were answered. The queen gave birth to twins: a boy, Lal Kamal, whose eyes shone like red lotus petals, and a girl, Neel Kamal, whose skin was the soft blue of a water lily.

The children grew up happy, their laughter echoing through the palace. The queen told them stories under the shade of the mango trees, while the king lifted them onto his shoulders as they watched the evening lamps drift down the river. But in a dark corner of the kingdom, a wicked sorceress named Kalo Chhaya watched with envy. Her heart was as black as the night. 'If I cannot have such blessings, neither shall they,' she muttered.

One moonless night, Kalo Chhaya crept into the palace. With a whispered curse and foul-smelling smoke, she snatched the sleeping twins.

'You'll never know happiness again!' she hissed.

She cast Lal Kamal far into a distant forest, turning him into a tiny red bird. Then she threw Neel Kamal into a stagnant pond, transforming her into a wilting blue lotus, guarded by her magic.

Lal Kamal, now a little red bird, flew for days. His tiny heart ached with a strange sadness. He landed on a tall sal tree, and chirped mournfully, a sound of deep loss.

One day, a wise old hermit passing by found the bird. 'This is no common bird,' he said. With gentle chants, he sprinkled holy water and in a flash of light, the bird became a boy again.

'Who am I?' Lal Kamal asked, confused. He remembered nothing of his past.

'You are a prince,' the hermit told him. 'And you seek your lost twin.'

Meanwhile, Neel Kamal, the blue lotus, slowly faded in the witch's pond. Her petals drooped, and her colour dulled. She felt a constant chill, a deep loneliness. The witch often visited, cackling.

'Soon you'll be nothing but dust!' Kalo Chhaya sneered at the wilting flower.

As Lal Kamal grew, his longing to find his twin intensified. He often heard the wind carry a faint tune, like the sigh of a sister calling. He knew he had to find the source of that song.

He set off on a perilous journey. He crossed treacherous rivers where unseen creatures lurked. He met strangers along the way, helping an old woman carry water, sharing food with hungry travellers, never turning aside from kindness.

'I must find her,' he murmured to himself, even though he didn't know who 'she' was.

Finally, he arrived at a dark, gloomy land. The air was heavy with the smell of decay. He found the stagnant pond, covered in green slime. There, almost hidden, was a fading blue lotus. He felt an immediate connection.

Just then, Kalo Chhaya appeared, her eyes burning. 'What are you doing here, boy?' she snarled.

THE LOTUS TWINS AND THE SORCERESS'S CURSE

Lal Kamal bravely confronted her. He remembered the hermit's words: 'Dark magic hides in dark jewels.' He saw a shimmering amulet around her neck. Summoning courage, he leapt forward.

'Your evil ends here!' he shouted. With both hands he tore the amulet from her neck and hurled it to the ground. It shattered beneath his heel.

As the amulet shattered, a brilliant light erupted. Kalo Chhaya shrieked, 'No! My power!' She dissolved into a cloud of black smoke, banished forever.

The stagnant pond instantly cleared. The blue lotus shimmered, then transformed into his beloved sister, Neel Kamal!

'Lal Kamal!' she cried, tears streaming down her face.

'Neel Kamal!' he shouted, embracing her tightly.

Together, Lal Kamal and Neel Kamal returned to their kingdom. The King and Queen, who had never given up hope, wept with happiness.

A grand celebration lasted for seven joyful days and seven lively nights. Musicians played cheerful tunes, and everyone danced.

Lal Kamal and Neel Kamal grew to become wise and kind. They never forgot the trials they had endured, nor the strength they had found in one another.

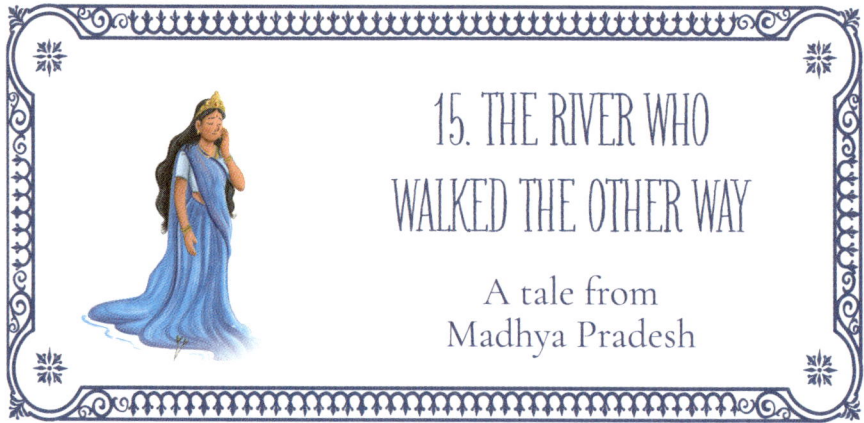

15. THE RIVER WHO WALKED THE OTHER WAY

A tale from Madhya Pradesh

Once in the forested hills of Amarkantak, a river spirit was born from the tears of Lord Shiva. Her name was Narmada.

She was unlike any other. Her voice was soft like water flowing over pebbles, and wherever she walked, green shoots burst from the ground. Birds followed her, calling sweet songs from the trees. The mountain breeze slowed down to listen to her hum. Even the tiger bowed his head when she passed.

All the rivers that flowed from those hills admired Narmada's grace. But none more than Sonbhadra, a strong and handsome river spirit who came roaring down from the northern stones. His waters thundered through the valleys, carrying a sound that rolled like drums across the land.

When Sonbhadra saw Narmada dancing by the waterfalls, he stopped in his tracks. Her smile was quiet, but her presence made the leaves tremble. He bowed low and said, 'Let us join our waters and flow together to the sea.'

Narmada, though shy, was curious. She had never seen such a powerful river. His voice was loud, but his eyes were kind. She nodded, and the forest began to prepare for their wedding. Deer trampled petals into the forest paths. Monkeys tied garlands of marigold. Even the clouds seemed to hold back their rain for the special day.

But among Narmada's companions was another river maiden called Juhila. She had long admired Sonbhadra's strength from afar. Her heart was restless and heavy with envy.

The night before the wedding, when the hills were asleep and fireflies blinked above the grass, Juhila crept away. She went to Sonbhadra and whispered soft promises. 'Come with me now,' she said, 'Why wait for morning?'

Sonbhadra, caught between desire and duty, followed her into the night.

When Narmada rose before sunrise and found them gone, she stood still by the cliff edge and watched the empty path. Her waters trembled, and the forest was silent around her.

The elders of the forest came to her. They brought honey and sweet fruit and tried to comfort her. 'The ocean still waits,' they said gently. 'You can follow your path and meet them there.'

But Narmada looked to the west, where the hills dipped low and the sky opened wide. Her heart no longer pointed towards the ones who had forgotten her worth.

But her trust had already been broken. And so, instead of turning east like the other rivers of the land, Narmada carved her way westward. Through thick jungle and black rock, she flowed alone, carrying with her the memory of truth and the strength to begin again.

As she passed through the heart of Madhya Pradesh, villages bloomed along her banks. Fishermen cast nets in her waters. Women bathed by her ghats and lit lamps in her name. Her waves told stories of pride and peace.

People began to call her Ma Narmada. Not because she followed the others, but because she taught them to walk with dignity.

Even now, when the sun rises over the Narmada and the sky turns gold, old women tell children why she flows west, away from where she was once meant to go. They say she is no ordinary river. She is a river who remembered who she was and chose her own way.

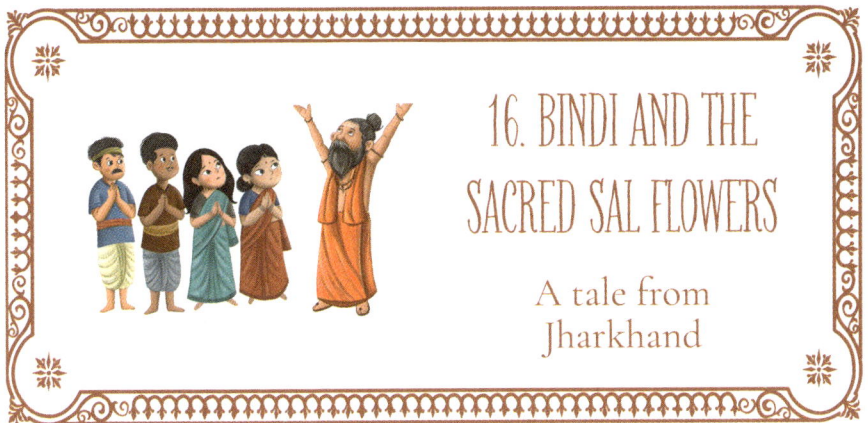

16. BINDI AND THE SACRED SAL FLOWERS

A tale from Jharkhand

In the green forests of Jharkhand, there lived a happy girl named Bindi. She was very special because she was the daughter of Mother Earth, but she lived with the Oraon tribe like their own child. Every morning, she woke up to the sounds of peacocks calling and leaves dancing in the wind.

'Good morning, beautiful trees!' Bindi would say as she walked through the forest. The village elders always smiled and said, 'Look how the flowers bloom brighter wherever Bindi goes!'

Even the shy deer and rabbits would come close to her because they knew she was kind. 'Hello, little friends,' she would whisper to them, and they would nod as if they understood every word.

Every day, Bindi would collect the golden sal flowers that fell from the tall trees. 'These flowers are gifts from Mother Earth,' she would tell the other children.

She would carry the flowers to the village temple. 'Please protect our village,' Bindi would pray as she placed the flowers at the god's feet.

All the villagers would gather around to watch. 'Thank you, Bindi,' they would say. 'The god loves your flowers.' Everyone felt safe and happy when Bindi brought the flowers.

One beautiful spring morning, when the sal trees had the loveliest flowers, Bindi went to collect them for a special prayer day. The forest was full of birds and bees. 'What a perfect day!' she said, filling her basket with the best flowers.

'I will take a bath in the pond before going to the temple,' Bindi decided. The pond water looked very special that day, glimmering in the morning sun. 'How beautiful the water looks!' she said.

As Bindi stepped into the cool water, something magical happened. The water began to glow brighter and brighter. 'Mother Earth is calling me home,' Bindi whispered with a smile. The golden water gently pulled her deeper, and she felt very peaceful and happy.

The villagers waited and waited for Bindi to come back with the flowers. 'Where is our dear Bindi?' they asked each other. When evening came, they went looking for her.

They found her bamboo basket by the pond, still full of fresh sal flowers, but Bindi was nowhere to be seen. 'Oh no! What happened to Bindi?' the villagers cried.

The wise village priest, who was very old and knew many secrets, understood what had happened. 'Do not cry,' he told everyone. 'Bindi has gone back to Mother Earth, but she has left us a gift that will stay with the forest forever.'

The next day, something amazing happened. The sal trees had more beautiful flowers than ever before! 'Look!' said the children. 'The flowers are so much brighter now!'

'This is Bindi's gift to us,' explained the priest. 'Her spirit lives in every sal flower now.' The villagers picked the golden flowers, just as Bindi always did. When the villagers took these special flowers to the temple, they could feel Bindi's love and blessings with them.

The priest had a wonderful idea. 'Every spring, when the sal trees bloom, we will celebrate a festival called Sarhul,' he announced. 'We will offer the golden sal flowers to God and remember our dear Bindi.'

'What a lovely idea!' said all the villagers. 'We will never forget Bindi and her kindness.'

The story of Bindi and the magical sal flowers spread to

other villages in Jharkhand. 'We want to celebrate Sarhul too!' said the other tribes. Soon, everyone was celebrating this happy spring festival.

Even today, when spring comes to Jharkhand, the tribal people celebrate Sarhul with great joy. They gather the sweet-smelling sal flowers and offer them to their gods.

Every spring when the sal flowers bloom, the people of Jharkhand remember that kindness and love never truly disappear.

17. THE PEACOCK AND THE SALT MERCHANT OF KUTCH
A tale from Gujarat

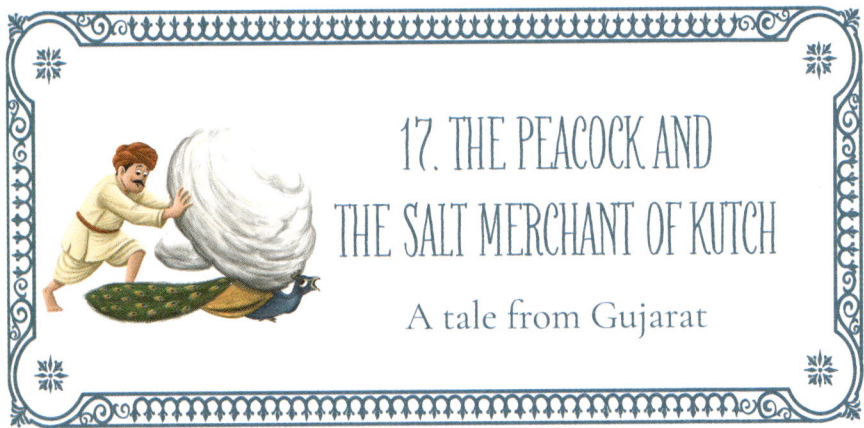

In the vast white expanse of the Rann of Kutch, lived a humble salt merchant named Kiran. He and his family lived in a small mud house with a thatched roof. His weathered hands bore the permanent stains of brine, and his cotton pagri was bleached white from years of working under the merciless sun. Each morning, he would load his wooden cart with salt crystals and take them to sell in faraway villages and markets.

The small village of Bhuj depended on Kiran's salt for their daily needs. The women would gather at the well each evening, chatting and pointing as they waited for his cart. The children ran ahead, eager to see the crystals piled high on the wooden cart.

One summer, the village of Bhuj was suffering from a great drought, and the fields lay cracked and empty. Kiran was collecting salt from the dried lake bed, when he heard a pitiful cry echoing across the empty landscape. Following the sound, he discovered a magnificent peacock trapped beneath a heavy chunk of salt rock. The bird's brilliant blue and green feathers were dulled with dust, and its tail was spread helplessly across the white ground.

Without hesitation, Kiran used his iron crowbar to lift the crushing weight, helping the poor bird out of its suffering. The peacock, finally pulling free, stretched its elegant neck and looked directly into Kiran's eyes.

THE PEACOCK AND THE SALT MERCHANT OF KUTCH

'Kind merchant,' the peacock spoke, 'you have saved my life when you could have left me to die in this dry salty land. I am no ordinary bird, but a magical creature of the desert. In return for your compassion, I shall grant you three wishes.'

Kiran's eyes widened with wonder, but he remained humble. 'Noble peacock, I seek nothing for myself. But if you have such power, I wish for rain to fall upon our dried up land. The wells of Bhuj have run dry and the children cry from thirst.'

The peacock spread its magnificent tail, and each feather eye seemed to glow with inner light. Immediately, dark clouds gathered in the clear sky, and rain began to fall upon the salt desert. Kiran watched in amazement as the dried earth drank deeply.

'For my second wish,' Kiran continued, 'I ask that the salt trade may prosper, so that the people of Kutch may never know poverty again.'

The peacock danced gracefully, its feet barely touching the ground, and suddenly the entire Rann began to shimmer with the finest salt crystals anyone had ever seen. Merchants from distant lands would travel for months to trade their gold for this magical salt of Kutch.

Now came the moment for Kiran's final wish. He thought of his own family. He thought of all the comforts and riches he could wish for. But then he remembered the peacock's words about kindness, and he looked across the vast landscape where his people had struggled for generations.

'Great peacock,' he said with quiet dignity, 'I wish for all the people to live in harmony with nature, respecting every creature that shares this land, so that the desert may bloom with life for generations to come.'

The peacock's cry of joy echoed across the entire Rann like a song of celebration. Its feathers blazed with rainbow colours, and a warm golden light spread across the desert. The peacock itself began to glow more brightly until it transformed into a beautiful woman, dressed in robes of peacock blue and emerald green.

'I am the guardian spirit of this land,' she revealed, her voice now like gentle rain on parched earth. 'For centuries, I have watched over the Rann, waiting for someone with a heart pure enough to understand that true wealth lies not in gold or silver, but in the balance between all living things.'

With a graceful gesture, she blessed Kiran and his descendants to always find prosperity through honest work and kindness to others. Then she slowly disappeared into the distance.

From that day forward, the salt of Kutch became renowned throughout the world, and the region prospered. But more importantly, the people learned to live in harmony with the desert, protecting the wildlife and sharing their good fortune with all who came to their land. During the monsoon season, when peacocks dance across the Rann, the people of Kutch remember Kiran's story and the wisdom of choosing compassion over greed.

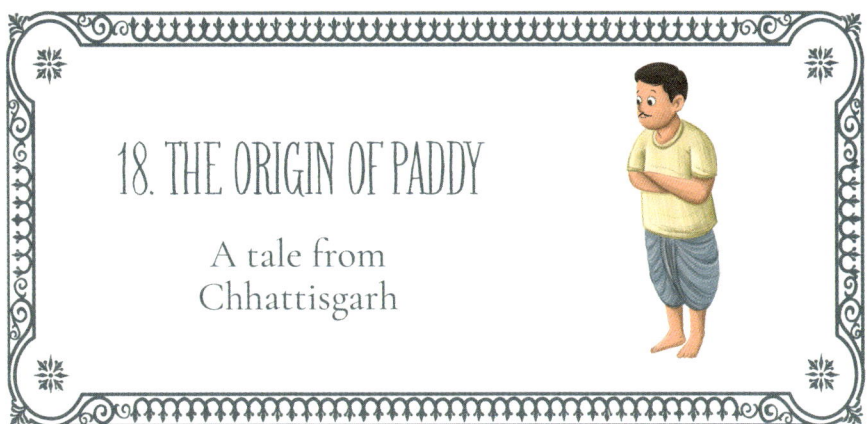

18. THE ORIGIN OF PADDY

A tale from Chhattisgarh

Long, long ago, before they started to grow rice in their fields, the people of Chhattisgarh lived on wild roots and forest fruits. They dug up tubers with sticks, plucked jamun from tall trees and hunted small animals for food. Life was hard, and people often went about half-bellied.

In a quiet village by the edge of the forest, there lived a poor farmer named Bhola. He had a little mud hut with a thatched roof and a patch of land full of stones. He worked from sunrise to sunset, but the earth was not kind to him. His harvests were always poor, and no matter how hard he worked, the grain he gathered was never enough. Still, Bhola was gentle, honest and never greedy. He always shared his meal of boiled roots with the birds and squirrels that visited his doorstep.

One evening, an old woman came to Bhola's hut. Her back was bent, and her white hair fell over her shoulders. She knocked softly on his door.

'Baba,' she said, 'I am tired and hungry. Will you give me something to eat?'

Bhola quickly lit a small fire, boiled the last of his roots and placed them on a leaf plate. He then gave her a gourd full of cool water.

The woman ate slowly, smiling after each bite. When she finished, she looked at Bhola and said, 'You are a kind man, Bhola. I am not just an old woman. I am a goddess in disguise. For your goodness, I will give you a gift.'

She reached into the folds of her cloth and took out a handful of golden grains.

'These are paddy seeds,' she said. 'Plant them in your field. Water them, care for them and never waste even a single grain of rice. If you respect food, your land will always stay full.'

Before Bhola could speak, the goddess vanished into the shadows of the forest.

Bhola followed her words with care. He planted the seeds, and within days, green shoots sprouted. Soon, the field turned golden, dancing in the wind like silk. Bhola harvested the rice carefully, saved the husks and swept up every grain from the floor.

The village watched in wonder. For the first time, someone had enough rice to cook fragrant khichdi, to make sweet kheer and to feed every hungry child.

But Bhola's neighbour, Laxman, was not pleased. He grew jealous. One night, he crept into Bhola's hut and stole a handful of paddy seeds.

Laxman planted them in his own field. The crops grew, just as before. But he did not respect the field like Bhola. He let the rice fall and rot. He threw away leftovers and laughed when birds came to eat.

That very night, a great wind blew across his fields. The rice plants withered. The grains turned to dust. By morning, his field was bare.

Laxman ran to Bhola, crying, 'Why did this happen?'

Bhola looked at the empty land and said gently, 'The goddess warned us. If we waste food, we lose its blessing.'

From that day, everyone in the village treated rice with care. They swept the floor after meals, fed leftovers to animals and never let a single grain go to waste.

THE ORIGIN OF PADDY

Even now, in Chhattisgarh, during harvest time, people place the first handful of rice before their home shrine and whisper prayers of thanks. Because they remember the story of Bhola, the kind farmer, and how rice came to be not just a crop, but a gift.

19. THE LEGEND OF CHILIKA LAKE
A tale from Odisha

There was a time when the sea near Puri was quiet, and the land where Chilika Lake now lies was dry and cracked. The breeze carried the sharp scent of salt and tamarind through a small village that stood near the shore. The sun scorched the red earth all day, turning the fields brittle and the paths hot.

At night, fishermen slept beside their nets, listening to the hush of the waves as they lapped gently against the coast. Children chased dragonflies through the coconut groves, while the temple bell rang at dusk.

But one day, a grave event shook the coast. A hundred black ships, which had sails tall as palm trees, crept towards the coast. Their wood was splintered and stained, their flags marked with skulls. The people in the village saw them in the distance, moving silently through the water.

They had heard of the man who sailed them. Raktabahu, the pirate king. He had heard stories about Puri's gold, idols and quiet riches. Finally, he had come for Puri.

Raktabahu stopped his fleet a little away from the coast. His men waited with swords in their teeth for the right moment to strike.

'At nightfall,' Raktabahu hissed, 'we march. No one will know until it is too late.'

THE LEGEND OF CHILIKA LAKE

But the sea was not still.

A soft current began to move in the sea, pulling gently at the ships tied near the shore. The water slipped past quietly, almost without a sound. Little things started floating away—like banana peels, a broken piece of metal and even a single sandal. The current carried them into the stream that flowed past the village, and from there all the way to the big town of Puri.

That evening, as women filled their pots, they found the water oily. A boy pulled out a feathered cap. A priest uncovered a broken blade.

'This is not a good sign,' said the old fisherwoman, her voice growing in concern. 'It is a warning from the ocean.'

Word spread like wind through dry leaves. The people of Puri gathered their children, took the temple idols and left the city dark and empty.

When night fell, Raktabahu and his men stepped ashore.

But there was no sign of anyone, anywhere. There were no guards. No cries. No lights in the homes. The pirate king frowned, unable to understand what was going on.

'They knew we were coming!' he growled. 'The sea has betrayed us.'

He turned to the waves behind him, roaring at them in anger. But then they began to notice that the tide had slowly started to rise.

'We walk through it!' he bellowed. 'We walk through and take what is ours!'

With weapons raised and rage in their hearts, the army followed. But the sea was listening.

First, a wind rose, sudden and sharp. Then the waves started to grow restless. The water began to rise quickly. It slapped against the pirates' armour and ankles, then knees, then hips. The sky darkened as clouds curled overhead like thick smoke.

Thunder cracked, and the sea roared. A giant wave rose like a mountain and crashed onto the men. Their ships were torn apart and Raktabahu vanished into the depths of the ocean.

When morning came, there was no sign of the army. But something had changed.

Where the earth had once been dry, a vast lake shimmered. White birds flew low over its calm surface. The fishermen returned to see the lake brimming with life.

'The sea has given us a gift,' whispered an old woman. 'She has swallowed the evil pirate army and gifted us a lake.' The fisherfolk called this lake Chilika. Even now, when storms sweep across the lake and waves crash against the shore, children press their ears to the windows and wonder:

'Is it only the wind? Or is it Raktabahu still shouting, deep below the waves?'

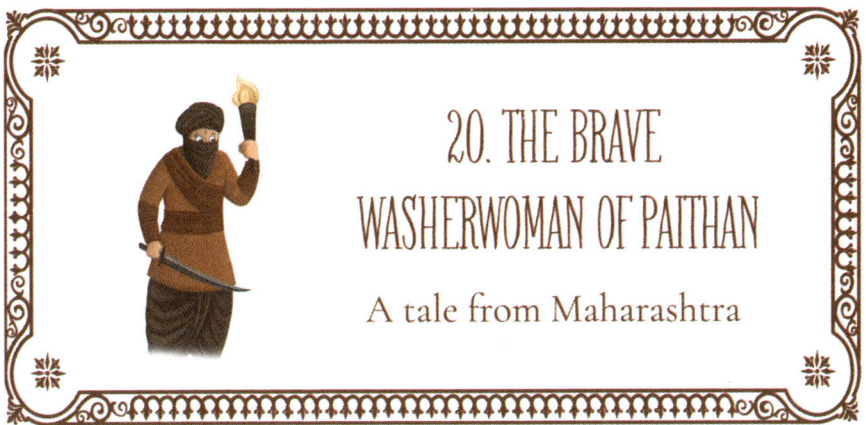

20. THE BRAVE WASHERWOMAN OF PAITHAN

A tale from Maharashtra

Beside the wide Godavari River stood the town of Paithan, lined by mango groves. In a stone house near the ghat lived Janki, the washerwoman. Every morning, she carried a bundle of clothes on her head and walked barefoot to the river. She scrubbed saris and dhotis against black stones, singing Lavani songs between each slap of cloth.

In her village, she was known for her kindness. She shared her lunch of bhakri and thecha with stray dogs and guided grandmothers down the slippery temple steps during monsoon.

One moonless night, while the whole village was asleep, trouble crossed the river. A gang of dacoits arrived by boat. They wore dark turbans and carried swords. Their leader held a red flag and pointed straight towards the temple, 'We're going to loot that temple and take everything that's worth a coin.'

The potter's boy dropped the clay pot he was carrying and tore through the narrow lanes, his feet slapping against the stones.

'Dacoits!' he cried, his voice cracking. 'They are crossing the river!'

Doors opened with a creak. Mothers pulled children into their arms.

One man shouted, 'Bar the doors! Do not go out!'

Another whispered, trembling, 'We cannot face swords with bare hands.'

A group of villagers ran towards the banyan grove, hoping its roots would hide them, while others bolted their shutters tight. Fear settled over the town like a heavy fog.

But Janki stayed where she was.

She tied her wet hair in a knot, tightened her sari and marched to the street. She had no weapon, only her laundry stones and a steady heart.

She ran to the ghat and picked up two brass plates. She slammed them together with such force that the sound bounced across the river like temple drums in festival season.

'Who is that?' a villager whispered from a window.

'It's Janki,' came the hushed reply.

Then she lit every diya she could find and placed them along the road, one by one, as though a whole battalion were arriving.

She climbed the temple steps, raised her arms and shouted,

'We are ready. Come if you dare. Paithan's women do not hide from shadows.'

Dogs barked, and the sound of banging plates echoed through the night. The bandits paused. The flickering torches made the narrow street look alive with movement. The clanging sounded like swords. Shadows grew taller than they were.

'There are too many,' one muttered, shifting his grip on the sword.

Another dacoit peered at the glowing lamps and hissed, 'I see shadows moving—dozens of them. They are waiting for us.'

The leader clenched his jaw, trying to appear fearless, but his fingers tightened around the red flag. He squinted at the narrow street lit with rows of flickering diyas, the clanging of plates ringing like a war drum in his ears.

For a moment, even he wondered if a whole army had gathered behind the temple walls.

'It is a trap,' whispered the leader. 'They are waiting.'

And without a fight, they fled.

By morning, the news of Janaki's brave act spread through the town. Children danced in the streets. Women tied flowers in

THE BRAVE WASHERWOMAN OF PAITHAN

Janki's hair. The temple priest placed a garland of tulsi around her neck and declared, 'She is Janki, the warrior of Paithan.' From then on, her tale travelled with wandering singers and tamasha troupes.

And even today, elders of Paithan say, 'Bravery wears many faces. It does not always ride a horse or carry a sword. Sometimes, it wears a wet sari, carries a washing stone and answers fear with fire.'

21. THE FARMER AND THE TALKING BULL
A tale from Telangana

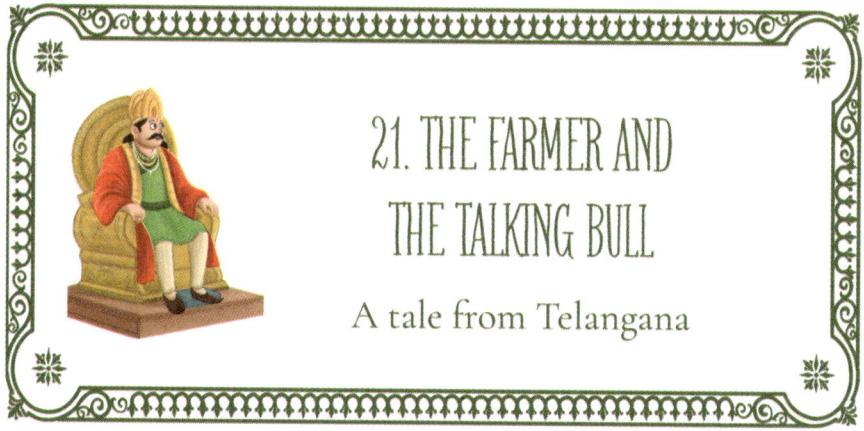

There was once a time, when the winds over the Deccan plateau carried stories, and one of them was about a farmer named Raju. His house was made of clay, his clothes were simple and his feet were always bare. He didn't have much, but he had one treasure—his bull, Bheemudu.

Bheemudu was no ordinary bull. His coat was dark and shiny, and his horns curved like crescent moons. Day after day, he pulled the plough through the stubborn earth.

Raju loved his land, though it was small, and he took care of Bheemudu like a beloved pet. But times were hard. The sun grew hotter. The ground cracked. Still, Raju worked from sunrise to moonrise, and Bheemudu ploughed beside him without rest.

One night, Raju was returning from the village market when something strange happened. Bheemudu lifted his head, blinked his wise brown eyes and spoke.

'Master,' he said, his voice deep and steady, 'you toil without pause. Your bones ache. Your hands bleed. Let me go to the king and ask for a day of rest.'

Raju dropped his clay cup. His mouth fell open. For a moment Raju thought he was dreaming. How could a bull speak? After the first shock passed, Raju steadied himself and answered Bheemudu.

THE FARMER AND THE TALKING BULL

Raju sat down on the mud floor, still shaken. 'But... the palace is far, Bheemudu. And what if the guards laugh? What if the king is angry?'

Bheemudu lowered his great head. 'Then let them laugh. I am not afraid. You have given me food and care all my life. Now let me give you rest.'

Raju's eyes filled with tears. He stroked the bull's neck and whispered, 'If you believe the king will listen, then go. You carry not just my hope, but the hope of every farmer.'

He stood, took a garland of marigolds and gently placed it around Bheemudu's neck. 'Go, my friend. May your words be stronger than my tired hands.' The next morning, the village stirred with whispers as Bheemudu walked through the streets, a red silk cloth tied around his shoulders. Everyone watched as Bheemudu walked all the way to Hyderabad, to the king's palace. At the gates, the guards froze in surprise. They had never seen a bull walk into the palace. Inside the court, the king sat on a throne carved from sandalwood. His beard was white, and his eyes sharp.

'What is this?' he asked. 'A bull who can speak?'

Bheemudu stepped forward and bowed low.

'Your Majesty,' he said, 'My master is a farmer who works hard every day in your fields. I do not ask for gold or gifts. I only ask that he be given one day each week to rest, so his back may not break and his heart may feel light again.'

The king was silent. Then he laughed with wonder.

'A talking bull asks for rest, not for himself but for his master. That is rare. Very well. Raju shall rest every seventh day. And for his honesty, I grant him two acres of fertile land beside the river.'

When Bheemudu returned, Raju wept with joy. From then on, Sundays became quiet and pleasant. Raju sat beneath the tamarind tree, listening to birdsongs. Bheemudu chewed sweet grass and sat by his master's side.

Soon, other farmers followed the same routine. They rested every sunday. Their body and mind healed. Their crops grew taller. Their animals lived longer. And that is how a bull's braveness brought rest and peace to the whole village.

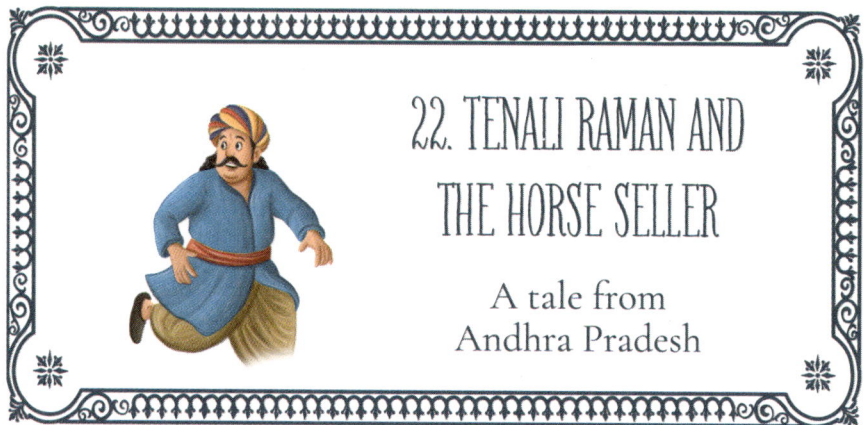

22. TENALI RAMAN AND THE HORSE SELLER

A tale from Andhra Pradesh

One bright morning in the kingdom of Vijayanagara, the sun rose over the roofs and temples of Hampi. At the heart of the town, the market was bustling with stalls selling colourful handloom cloth, clay pots and piles of red chillies.

Among the chatter of vendors and clang of temple bells stood a tall man with a crooked moustache and a silk turban. He scanned the whole market with a wicked smile. Tied beside him was a horse with its coat glimmering in the sun.

'Royal breed!' cried the man, slapping the horse's flank. 'Fast as a river! Trained by Persian warriors! Fit for kings and zamindars!'

The crowd stared, wide-eyed. Men stopped to look. Children sucking tamarind toffees giggled in curiosity.

Just then, Tenali Raman arrived. Clad in a simple cotton dhoti with a red tilak on his forehead, he smiled.

'How much for this fine fellow?' he asked, reaching out to pat the horse's smooth neck.

'One hundred gold coins,' replied the seller, his chest puffing up with pride. 'A fair price for a royal beast.'

Tenali squinted. 'Does it also do kuchipudi dances?'

The crowd burst into giggles. The seller forced a smile. 'It gallops like a drumbeat, if that's what you mean.'

TENALI RAMAN AND THE HORSE SELLER

'One hundred gold coins is no small sum,' Tenali said, tapping his chin. 'Why, with that much I could buy a field, a house, and still have money left for sweets.'

The seller snapped, 'Can a field carry you across rivers? Can a house race faster than the wind? This horse is no ordinary animal!'

'True,' Tenali nodded. 'But how do I know it won't stumble at the first stone or refuse to move after the first mile?'

The seller threw out his chest. 'Impossible! Its hooves are strong, and its breath never tires. You doubt me? Ask the crowd—look at this beauty!'

'Crowds can be fooled,' Tenali replied calmly. 'But I trust my own eyes. Let me test it, and tomorrow I'll return with your hundred gold coins.'

'No, no,' the seller spluttered. 'It's not a rental bullock cart! You buy, you pay!'

'But surely a noble animal deserves a noble trial,' said Tenali, raising one eyebrow.

The seller, now watched by half the market, could not back down. 'Fine! Take it. But return it by sunset, or pay me in full!'

'Agreed,' said Tenali. He climbed on and rode away through the narrow lanes.

The day passed. The sun climbed high. The seller waited. He chewed betel leaves to calm himself and kept glancing towards the road.

Evening came. The skies blushed orange. Still no horse.

Just before sunset, Tenali strolled into the market—on foot.

'Where's my horse?' the seller cried.

'It ran off,' Tenali said with a shrug. 'Leapt into a chilli field and vanished near a toddy palm. I even called out in Telugu, but it wouldn't return.'

'Then pay me!'

'Why should I?' said Tenali. 'I said I'd pay if I kept it. Clearly, the horse had other plans.'

The crowd roared with laughter. The seller's face turned dark.

Just then, two palace guards stepped forwards. 'We've been

searching for this thief. That horse was stolen from the royal stables in Amaravati!'

The man spun around to flee, but his foot slipped on a puddle and he crashed to the ground. As the guards hauled him away, Tenali bowed. 'Remember, friends, not every shining turban hides a wise head.' The market clapped and cheered. And with a chuckle, Tenali walked into the evening crowd.

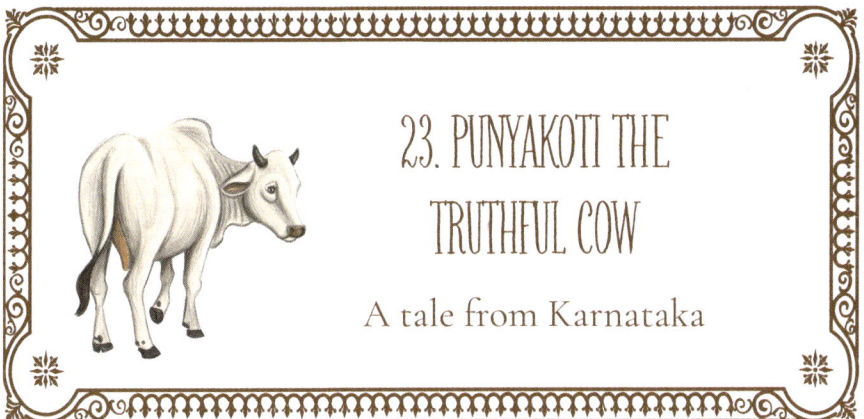

23. PUNYAKOTI THE TRUTHFUL COW

A tale from Karnataka

In a quiet village near the edge of the Bandipur forest, there lived a cow named Punyakoti. She belonged to a kind cowherd who let her graze freely in the meadows every day.

Everyone in the village knew Punyakoti. She never pushed the other cows, never wandered where she shouldn't and never stole from another's patch of grass. She was known far and wide as the most honest creature in the herd.

One golden afternoon, while grazing near the edge of the forest, Punyakoti followed a trail of fresh green shoots and wandered deeper than usual. The trees began to get thicker as she went deeper. The air smelled of moss and damp leaves. Suddenly, with a rustle and a roar, a tiger sprang out from behind a tree.

'I am starving,' he growled, his yellow eyes locked on hers. 'And you are going to be my meal.'

Punyakoti trembled with fear. She bowed her head politely. 'Dear tiger, I understand. But I have a little calf waiting at home. Let me feed her one last time, and I promise I will return to you.'

The tiger blinked in surprise. 'You expect me to believe that? You'll just run away like the others.'

'I am not like the others,' said Punyakoti softly. 'They may run, but I will not. I have never lied, not even to my calf. Why would I lie to you?'

The tiger's tail twitched. 'Why should I care for your honesty? Hunger does not wait for promises.'

'Hunger will not leave you,' said Punyakoti, her eyes steady, 'but if you eat me now, my calf will starve. If you let me go, both of us will have peace—my calf with her meal, and you with mine when I return.'

The forest fell silent. Something about the cow's voice, so steady and kind, made the tiger agree.

'Go,' he said. 'But if you do not return, I will come looking for you.'

Punyakoti trotted home as fast as her legs could carry her. Her calf was waiting by the fence, crying for milk. She nuzzled the little one, fed her gently, then licked her forehead one last time.

The cowherd called out, 'Where are you going, Punyakoti? Stay with your calf!'

Punyakoti turned back, her eyes heavy with sorrow, and said softly, 'I made a promise to the tiger than I would return to him.'

The cowherd dropped his stick in shock. 'Are you mad, Punyakoti? Who makes a promise to a beast like that? He will devour you!'

'Better to keep my word and lose my life,' Punyakoti replied, 'than to save my life and lose my truth.'

The calf tugged at her side, bleating. 'Amma, don't go! Stay with me.'

Her heart ached, but she bent and whispered, 'My little one, learn from me. A promise is sacred. Even if I do not return, the truth will protect you one day.'

She returned to the forest, bidding farewell to her child and to the whole herd. The tiger was still waiting, pacing beside the rocks.

'You came back,' he whispered. 'No one ever comes back.'

'I told you I would,' she replied.

The tiger looked at her, then lowered his head to the ground.

'I cannot eat you,' he said. 'You have shown me something I never knew—how strong truth can be.'

PUNYAKOTI THE TRUTHFUL COW

Ashamed of all the fear he had caused in the world, the tiger walked away. With one last look at the brave cow, he turned away and walked slowly into the forest, choosing to leave behind his cruel ways and never trouble the village again.

Punyakoti stood still for a long moment. Then she turned, walked back to her village and lay beside her calf in the warm evening light.

From that day on, the elders in the village told her story to every child, every herder and every traveller who passed by.

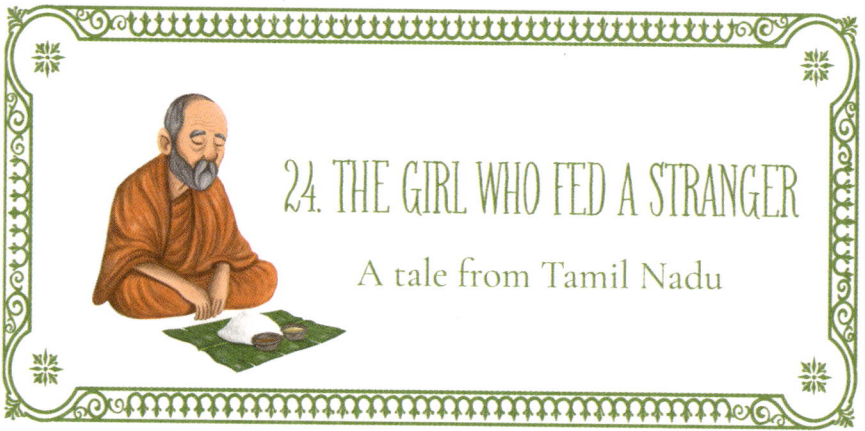

24. THE GIRL WHO FED A STRANGER

A tale from Tamil Nadu

Long ago, in the sun-baked village of Valliyur, there lived a landlord named Raghavan. His house stood tall with carved wooden pillars, golden lamps in every corner and rice barns bursting with grain. His fields stretched far beyond the nearby hills.

But Raghavan was stingy and unkind. Even though he was rich beyond measure, he never shared anything. His servants moved quickly, afraid to upset him. Poor people came to his gate asking for food or water, but they were always sent away. Even travellers who stopped by were turned back without kindness.

One summer morning, a wandering sage arrived at Valliyur's edge. His hair was tangled and matted, robes dusty from the many miles travelled and he leaned heavily on a worn wooden staff. Barefoot, he moved through the village, murmuring prayers and blessing each doorstep with gentle hands.

When he reached Raghavan's house, the sage paused beneath the spreading neem tree. 'Sir,' he said softly, 'I have walked many miles and ask only for a little rice and buttermilk to ease my hunger.'

Raghavan's face twisted with scorn. 'This is no temple. Beg elsewhere,' he snapped, turning sharply away.

The sage looked at him calmly. 'Do you not fear that riches without kindness are like wells without water?'

THE GIRL WHO FED A STRANGER

'My riches are mine,' Raghavan retorted. 'I earned them, I guard them. Why should I waste them on strangers?'

The sage shook his head gently. 'You guard gold as if it will last forever. Remember, even mountains crumble one day.'

Raghavan laughed harshly. 'Your riddles won't fill my stomach. Go, before I lose patience.'

The sage bowed his head and pressed a pinch of sacred ash at the foot of the gate. A fine dust shimmered faintly in the sunlight. Then he walked on without a word.

That night, strange things began to happen in Raghavan's house. The golden oil in the lamps thickened and blackened, making the flames flicker and die. The rice in the barns crumbled to dust, spilling softly like snow on the floor. Raghavan's heavy gold rings slipped from his fingers and broke apart like brittle leaves.

Each night, the curse deepened. The house grew colder. The shadows lengthened and deepened in the corners. Even the birds that nested in the eaves flew away in silence. The villagers whispered in fearful voices, 'The sage cursed him.'

Inside, Raghavan paced angrily, but his pride would not let him seek help. His daughter, Meenakshi, watched quietly. She was kind and gentle, unlike her father. She lit the few lamps left, swept the courtyard and gave the cows the last handfuls of hay. Often, she pressed her palm to the sacred ash at the gate hoping for a sign.

One afternoon, as dark clouds gathered over the hills and the first drops of rain began to fall, a wandering monk arrived at Raghavan's gate.

Before he could speak, Meenakshi brought him a banana leaf filled with steaming rice, thick sambar and cool buttermilk. 'Please eat, Swami,' she whispered, her voice steady but warm.

The monk smiled softly. After he finished, he rose and pulled a small pouch from his robe. He scattered tiny shimmering grains over the doorstep. The grains caught the fading light like fallen stars.

'Kindness lives here,' he said quietly. 'Let it grow and heal.'

That night, rain washed over Valliyur, pattering on leaves and roofs. The oil lamps flickered back to life. The barns filled once more with the scent of fresh grain. This made Raghavan see things differently, and he began to change his ways. He chose to leave his unkind ways behind and do good to for everyone.

From that day forward, Meenakshi welcomed every traveller, sage or stranger, with a bowl of food and a generous heart. The children of Valliyur sang songs of the girl who broke a curse with a simple meal and a kind spirit.

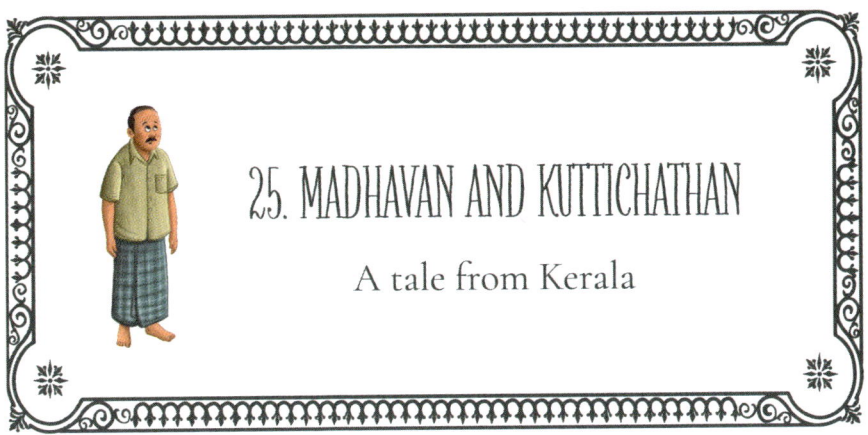

25. MADHAVAN AND KUTTICHATHAN

A tale from Kerala

In a small village along the backwaters of Kerala, lived a poor weaver named Madhavan. His hands were rough from years of hard work, weaving cloth so plain that few came to buy it.

There was a story the people of that village always whispered. The story of Kuttichathan, the red-eyed spirit who could slip into shadows like smoke. Some said he was a boy, others a black cat, but all knew he punished the greedy and the cruel. His laughter was a warning, sharp and echoing through the dark.

One evening, Madhavan was working by his flickering oil lamp. Suddenly, a chilling giggle floated through the open window. A small boy with wild black hair and glowing red eyes stood on the rooftop, grinning wide.

'Good evening, Madhavan,' said the boy with a smile.
Madhavan blinked. 'Who are you, child? I've never seen you before.'
'I am Kuttichathan,' the boy replied.
Madhavan's hands grew cold. 'Kuttichathan? The spirit?'
'Yes,' the boy said calmly. 'Don't be afraid.'
Madhavan swallowed hard. 'Then why have you come to me?'
The boy's eyes glowed brighter. 'I offer a gift. I will give you magic threads to weave the finest cloth. But you must promise to be

fair and kind to all who help you. But if you break your word, I will return and take it back from you.'

Madhavan hesitated. 'Magic... threads? Why me? I am only a poor man.'

'Because the poor often forget kindness when wealth enters their hands,' said Kuttichathan. 'I want to see if you will remember.'

Madhavan's voice trembled as he swore, 'I promise on my children's lives.'

In the cold dawn, a bundle of shining threads lay at his door. They shimmered like moonlight and felt softer than the morning mist. Madhavan worked day and night. His hands flew over the loom, weaving cloths glowing with colours no one had seen before. The village gathered, amazed. His fortunes changed for the better. His days of poverty were behind him, and he lived in comfort.

But little by little, greed began to creep into his heart Madhavan began to raise prices and pay his helpers less.

One of his helpers protested, 'Master, we worked all day and night, yet you give us only a handful of rice. This is not fair.'

A whisper rose from the shadows, cold and cruel, 'You broke your promise. Fairness brings fortune. Greed brings ruin.' Madhavan snapped, 'Do you think magic comes cheap? Be glad you even have work under my roof!'

One stormy night, a black cat with fiery eyes slipped silently into his courtyard. It prowled through the room, knocking over baskets and tangling threads. By morning, Madhavan's precious cloth was torn and his coins had vanished.

Madhavan woke up at dawn and gasped when he saw the ruin.

'Why do you punish me?' Madhavan cried, his voice breaking.

A whisper rose from the shadows, cold and cruel, 'You broke your promise. Fairness brings fortune. Greed brings ruin.' Madhavan fell to his knees. 'Forgive me, Kuttichathan! Give me one more chance. I will change. I swear it!'

The next day, Madhavan sought out the helpers he had cheated. He returned what he owed and worked humbly by their side. Slowly, the magic returned to his cloth and happiness returned to his home. From that day on, Madhavan never forgot Kuttichathan, the spirit who taught him justice.

OTHER BOOKS IN THE SERIES

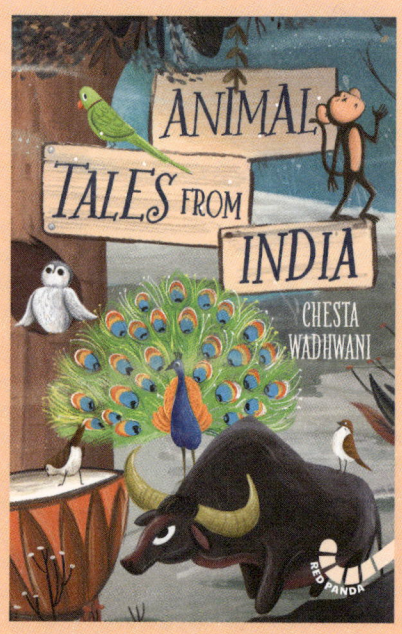
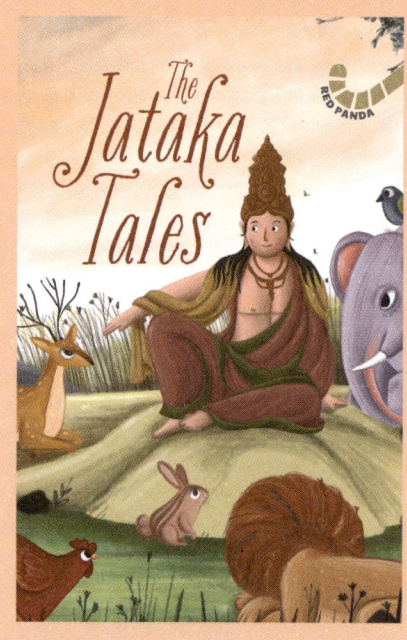